WHAT

also by Pheme Perkins
published by Paulist Press

HEARING THE PARABLES OF JESUS
LOVE COMMANDS IN THE NEW TESTAMENT
MINISTERING IN THE PAULINE CHURCHES
READING THE NEW TESTAMENT
THE GNOSTIC DIALOGUE

What We Believe

A Biblical Catechism of the Apostles' Creed

by

Pheme Perkins

PAULIST PRESS
New York/Mahwah

NIHIL OBSTAT:
Rev. Walter J. Edyvean, S.T.D.

IMPRIMATUR:
Bernard Cardinal Law

December 23, 1985

The *nihil obstat* and *imprimatur* are official declarations that a book or pamphlet is free of doctrinal or moral error. No implication is contained therein that those who have granted the *nihil obstat* and *imprimatur* agree with the contents, opinions or statements expressed.

Library of Congress
Catalog Card Number: 85-62875

ISBN: 0-8091-2764-4

Published by Paulist Press
997 Macarthur Boulevard
Mahwah, New Jersey 07430

Printed and bound in the
United States of America

Contents

Introduction

What Is Believing?

Now that you are older there are many things you thought were true that you now know are not. What are some of those things? Santa Claus? Maybe you didn't want to tell your mother or father that you knew that Santa Claus didn't come in a sleigh with presents, because you weren't sure if you'd get a Christmas present anymore. If you have younger brothers or sisters, maybe you have fun pretending to be Santa for them—or maybe for some other children who are not as fortunate as you are. If you do, then you have found out something. "Santa Claus" is about a very special spirit of giving, not about "getting things."

A "Santa Claus" present is not the kind of present that says, "Now you owe me one in return." It is a real gift, a surprise, an answer to a hope or a wish. It reminds us that "someone cares" for us. We know that we should show our gratitude for such a gift, so we sometimes leave something out for Santa to eat . . . We

1

might have been told to "be good" around Christmas time or "Santa won't come." That way the "gift" also taught us that caring and giving gifts are a response to something good in the other person. When we play Santa for poorer children whom we do not even know, we are pointing out something good about those people too. God cares for them. God feels their pain and loneliness. But God also asks us to reach out in love and sharing to others.

How Do We Believe?

The example about Santa Claus shows that there are two very different ways of believing. First, there's the kind of belief that we outgrow as we get older. That's a belief that there is a man in a red suit with a sleigh full of presents and a workshop at the North Pole. The world is a magical place where wishes come true. But we do not have to be very old before we see pictures of the North Pole, learn about airplanes and decide there can't be a Santa out there. That's when we start to learn the second kind of belief. That is belief that "someone cares" in the world, that people can and should be kind and generous to each other. We may even learn that "giving" and surprising someone else is as much fun as "getting things." Others may surprise us with their gifts in return.

You also learned that "being good" is more than a trade to get a reward of some kind. It is a response to the love and care which others have given us. We are not meant to "hate" being good, though sometimes it asks us to make an effort when we don't feel like it. We are meant to see ourselves as part of the larger spirit of love and goodness in the world. Believing means trusting in that love and goodness. It also means showing that you trust by the way you live.

Of course, we aren't asked to ignore all the bad things in the world. The Christmas story even reminds us that some of them happened to Jesus' family. The Jewish people were subject to a foreign power, the Romans. That is why there was a census being taken, so that the Roman governor could tax the Jewish people (Lk 2:1–2). Jesus' family had to flee from Judaea into Egypt in order to save the child's life (Mt 2:13–18). We are so used to thinking of taking a trip as a vacation and a time for having fun that we forget that the journeys in the Bible are not like that at all. Journeys were times of danger. You were separated from your relatives and people who knew you. You had to depend upon the uncertain hospitality of strangers or the equally uncertain "inns." Luke tells us about Jesus being born and put in a feeding trough for animals because there wasn't any place in the local inn (Lk 2:7). Other dangers on journeys included robbers and other accidents or sickness.

All of the great signs that accompany Jesus' birth do not remove him and his family from the dangers of their life. We are told that Jesus grew up in Nazareth. Nazareth was a very small farming village. It had about 1,600 to 2,000 people. Most of the houses would have been one story houses with four or five rooms around a central courtyard. Many of the babies born would never even live to be as old as you are. But we see Mary and Joseph "believing," that is, trusting in what God told them about Jesus. Because they believed we all receive a very special gift. Jesus comes to show us what God's love for us is like. Jesus comes to bring us back to God when we have forgotten about God. Jesus comes to remind the world that God seeks peace among all people on earth.

Why Believe?

Did you ever have a Christmas (or a birthday) when you really wanted a certain present? You kept hinting to your mother or father. You tried to be as good as you could. But you still didn't get it. Maybe it cost too much. Maybe your mother or father didn't think you should have it. Maybe someone tried to get what you wanted but got the wrong thing. Was your Christmas (or birthday) ruined because you were so disappointed? Or did something else take its place to make your day happy? Were you mad because you'd put so much effort into "being good"? Or did you like the results of your efforts to be more helpful and responsible? Maybe your mother or father praised you or someone else thanked you or gave you a surprise treat.

Believing is something like that. We sometimes imagine that God is calculating everything and that when we get to heaven we'll be "paid off" for being good with a giant Christmas. But we can also think about it in a different way—more like the basis for the unexpected surprises of love and goodness that come to us when we don't really expect or deserve them. We really remember those. They make us feel happy about ourselves and the world. Maybe we even decide to do the same for someone else.

Just When You Least Expect It . . .

The other day, I saw an example of such a surprise. I was in downtown Chicago waiting to get on the bus to the airport. It was raining and about 36 degrees out and getting dark. As the bus pulled up, a boy about nine years old came out from the doorway of an office building to sell papers to the people getting on the bus. Most of us were in too much of a hurry to get out of the cold rain to bother fishing out any money for a paper. Then one man reached in his pocket and gave the boy a dollar for the 25 cent paper. He also complimented the boy for doing a good job at keeping the papers dry. You can imagine how happy that boy looked after that.

I learned a lesson too. All I thought about when I decided not to buy a paper was the bother of standing in the rain and fishing out the money. It would be so much easier to buy the paper at the dry newstand when I got to the airport. I didn't even ''see'' the boy trying to sell his papers in a cold rain. But the man who gave him the dollar did. And that's what Jesus tells us over and over again in the Gospels we should see in other people.

The Fullness of Time

In Mark's Gospel, Jesus begins his ministry by telling the people, ''The time has been fulfilled and the kingdom of God is at hand. Repent and believe in the Gospel'' (Mk 1:15). When the Bible talks about ''the time being fulfilled'' it means something very special. People were hoping for a new time of blessing and salvation from God. Jesus announces that it has come. The expression ''kingdom of God'' does not mean that God is going to set up a country and rule it like a human king. The Bible speaks of God's kingdom or God's rule because all people are being called upon to accept God as the Lord. It is God's word that should set the basis for our lives and not some other authority. But we can't believe unless we ''repent.'' That word means to change our mind or our heart. In a way, we are never finished repenting. The lesson I learned on the Chicago street corner was about repenting—learning to see things God's way instead of my own way.

The Challenge To Believe

Why believe, then? It's not just because of some rewards that we expect in heaven. It's not just because my parents and a lot of my friends go to church, and it would seem funny if I didn't. It's not because religion is some sort of magic protection against ''bad things happening to you.'' Even Jesus had to suffer the ''hard times'' of growing up in a small, poor village and in a country that was dominated by an outside power. Indeed, Jesus even goes further than that. Jesus is willing to suffer and offer his life for other people. It's because God has shown us something in Jesus. God has shown us that we can live our lives on the basis of trust, hope and love for others.

Believing is a challenge. It is a challenge to "repent," to change our way of thinking and acting. It's the kind of challenge that takes up your whole life. You can never tell when you will need to learn a new lesson about faith or trust in God, about hope for the future, or about loving others as God loves you. Believing can be hard work. It's also full of surprises. In fact, we might even say to someone, "I dare you to believe . . . and to hope . . . and to love."

Learning To Believe

Believing is not something that is just spontaneous. We learn about believing from those around us. When we were baptized our parents and godparents took responsibility for introducing us to the Christian faith. We were made part of a community of people who share that faith. Ever since that time other people have been teaching us lessons about believing. What they say and what they do tell us about what faith and hope and love mean to them. Some of the examples of "believing" that we have seen may not have been very good ones. They may not focus very much on the spirit of trusting and loving God and other people that we find in Jesus.

Other examples may be very good indeed. Some of them may even come at times and in places we don't expect. While you are a child, adult Christians are responsible for seeing that you have good models for believing. When you are confirmed, you will be telling the other Christians with whom you live that you are old enough to be responsible for your own belief. That doesn't mean that other people will stop teaching and helping you to become a better Christian. We need other Christians to help us all our life.

Different Expressions of Belief

Most religions have some form of belief or trust in God. They also have some ideals for "being good" and showing mercy and compassion toward others. We belong to a special community of faith which takes its belief from the Bible and especially from the revelation of God in Jesus Christ. That's part of what we celebrate when we celebrate Christmas. Jewish people who do not believe in Jesus as the revelation of God do not celebrate Christmas. They have a celebration at about the same time of year, Hannukah. It celebrates a victory in which the sacred temple in Jerusalem was liberated from pagan conquerors and restored for worship of God. Sometimes the two celebrations can be confusing. A few weeks ago a five year old Jewish boy, who had finally understood that Jews didn't celebrate Christmas, was gazing at the Valentines in a local card store. He pleadingly asked his mother, "Mom, do we have Valentine's Day?" She said, "Yes," and they went inside to buy a card.

This little boy was trying to sort out the difference between special Jewish or Christian holidays and holidays that he could share with all of his playmates. By next year he will probably have sorted out the kids in his first grade class into those who celebrate Christmas and those who are like him and celebrate Hannukah. He will have a sense that he belongs to a different community of faith from other children. His Christian playmates, in turn, will also have learned that he's different.

When we are little, it's the special things we do, the religious holidays and celebrations that make us different. They set us apart from people who belong to a different faith. Even among those who are Christians, there are different churches. They have different styles of worship. In the Catholic Church, we have a celebration of the Mass, of Jesus' last meal with his disciples, every Sunday. Many other churches do not. Their usual Sunday service may be prayers, hymns, reading from the Bible and a sermon, which is usually much longer than the one in a Catholic church. Some of those churches will have a service of Communion or the Lord's Supper once a month. Some may only have it a few times a year. Those churches place their emphasis on reading the Bible and hearing it preached. In the Catholic Church, we emphasize the importance of coming close to God in Communion. We believe that God's presence in Communion helps us to carry out the word of God, which we hear read at the beginning of Mass.

As soon as we are told enough to start asking questions, we begin to learn about believing in another way. We not only see what people around us do and try to copy the behavior of parents or older children, we also ask to be told. Parents, teachers and priests start to explain things about Christianity. They may tell us stories from the Bible. We may see stories on TV, especially at Christmas and Eastertime. We may go to special classes either at our church or at school. Just as you need to know something about the story and traditions of America to be an American, you need to know about the story and traditions of your church.

You can always know more about your country as you get older. When I was in Chicago, I met a woman whose husband's hobby is a very special way of learning about America. He collects stamps, especially those issued in the South during the Civil War. She told me she wasn't very interested at first. But now she has learned that you can tell a whole history of our country from stamps. You can also always learn more about your faith. Many churches have special study groups for adults. During the summer many Catholic colleges conduct one and two week courses that people can take. And there are Catholic newspapers, magazines and book clubs. Some Catholics go to special weekends for a retreat to reflect on their faith and to learn to grow in it. There are weekends with a special purpose like preparing young couples for marriage or helping married couples strengthen their marriage. Still other adults may keep on growing in their faith by taking an active part in something connected with the Church.

You have already changed a lot from the time you were five or six. You can read and write. You can throw a ball and probably ride a bike. You can go some places on your own without an adult supervising you. Maybe you are even like my niece, who announced on her thirteenth birthday, "Only three more years until I can get my driver's license!" (Actually, she has to wait until she is sixteen and a half for a restricted license and eighteen for an unrestricted one.) At the rate she is going, she will even have money saved up for a car by the time she is that age. I don't think she'll change her mind in the next three years. She comes from a family of car lovers. When she was younger, she couldn't plan that far ahead. Now she is starting to have all sorts of plans. What plans do you have for yourself?

The Development of Faith

Just as you change and grow up, your faith changes too. If you are going to grow up as a Christian, you need to know more about what Christians believe than you did when you were five or six. The things you are learning in school now are the building blocks for what you will be learning later on. The things you learn about your faith now are the building blocks for the kind of Christian you will be in the future. This afternoon I was talking to one of my students. She is about to graduate from college and is going to go to Central America with a volunteer program for a year to help the poor people there. I asked her how she got interested in doing that. She hadn't been involved in any similar activities at college. She told me that it was really the example of her parents when she was in junior high and high school. Their family used to help out at a camp for kids with cerebral palsy in the summers. That was part of the way she learned what being a Catholic meant to her parents. Now she wants to try it out for herself in this volunteer program before she comes back to go to law school.

Even if you never do anything that dramatic, you still need to have a good start in understanding what Christians believe.

"What We Believe"

This book is an explanation of what we believe. It is based on a very old statement of Christian beliefs drawn up in the Roman Church over 1,500 years ago. This statement is called "The Apostles' Creed." It was used to teach new converts to Christianity the basics of their faith before they were admitted to the Church in baptism.

We will explain each of the beliefs referred to in the Creed using examples from the Bible, especially from the Gospels and the letters of Paul. We are not going to just file away a list of things to believe. We are going to see how those beliefs are part of the basic Christian story. And we are going to ask ourselves how a person who believes what the Creed teaches would act. Believing is not just having some opinions. It also means trying to act in ways that show others who we are.

The Apostles' Creed

I believe
in God the Father Almighty
Creator of heaven and earth;
and in Jesus Christ
his only Son, our Lord,
who was conceived by the Holy Spirit,
born from the virgin Mary,
suffered under Pontius Pilate,
was crucified, died and was buried, descended to hell.
On the third day he rose again from the dead,
ascended to heaven,
sits at the right hand of God, the Father almighty,
thence he will come to judge the living and the dead.
I believe in the Holy Spirit,
the holy catholic church,
the communion of saints,
the remission of sins,
the resurrection of the flesh,
and eternal life.

1

God: The Creator

*God the Father Almighty,
Creator of heaven and earth;*

Believing in God

At the time the Bible was written almost everyone in the world believed in gods and goddesses. They often made paintings and statues of the gods and goddesses and told stories about their behavior which made them look and act like powerful human beings. Sometimes the different gods and goddesses would be at odds with each other. The great revolution in the Bible was the announcement that there was only one God, not many. This basic faith is embodied in a classic Jewish confession of faith:

Hear, O Israel. The Lord our God is *one* Lord (Dt 6:4).

God Is Everywhere

In order to make it clear that their God was not like the humanized gods of the pagans, the Jews had commandments that prohibited making any statues or images to represent God. If you were to go inside a Roman temple, you would find statues of the god or goddess in whose honor the temple had been built. But there were no statues inside the Jewish temple in Jerusalem. God is present without any statues. God's presence is represented by the scrolls of the law, which embodies God's promises to Israel and God's revelation of how the people are to live.

God Is One

When the apostles began to preach the Gospel to people who were not Jews (called "Gentiles"), the first thing they had to do was to teach them that there was only one God. Then they could teach them that God had sent Jesus. Here is a brief passage from a letter Paul wrote to converts in Thessalonica (an area in northern Greece). It is in the form of a "mini-creed." It expresses what it meant for them to believe in Paul's message:

> You turned to God from idols, to serve a living and true
> God, and to wait for God's Son from heaven, whom
> God raised from the dead, Jesus who delivers us from
> the wrath to come (1 Thess 1:9–10).

You can find all of the themes of this creed reflected in the Apostles' Creed. When we say that we "believe in God," we mean that we believe in the one who is truly God.

Of course, most of us do not live in a country in which people still worship many gods and goddesses. The "God" of our creed is also the God revealed to Moses, the God of the Jewish people. But Christians claim that God has a special relationship to Jesus.

That belief in Jesus separates us from our Jewish friends who also believe in the God of Abraham and Moses.

The Challenge To Believe

The challenges to believing in God today come from people who claim that there is no God. The teaching of communist countries says that "God" is a false idea. People who believe in God are more willing to be victims of injustice and oppression because they think that God will reward them in heaven. These countries teach their children that the only thing worth devoting their lives to is the struggle to achieve the ideals of the communist state. If the communist system were completely worked out, people would no longer need to believe in God.

It is easy to identify the attack on God that comes from communist beliefs. But there is also an attack on God that lives in our Western, consumer-oriented society. We begin to think that the only things which matter are material things. Whatever we can possess is what counts. We may even think of people that way. They are objects to be used and then thrown away when we don't like them anymore or when they are too old or useless to us. Maybe you can even think of some people you know who seem to treat their friends like "things." They make friends with another kid because that kid has something they want to use. But when they are no longer interested in what that person has or can do for them they drop that friend and take up with someone else. People complain that they get treated like objects in other ways too. Our society can be very automated and impersonal. We don't know the people we do business with in stores. Everything is owned by something bigger. Even your boss doesn't have any real power to hire or fire you. She or he has to clear it with someone else. Burger King ads try to capitalize on our frustration with the impersonal "fast food" by proclaiming: "Have it your way."

What does an impersonal society have to do with not believing in God? God is not a "thing" that can be packaged and marketed. We have already seen that Christianity expects us to be involved with people, with caring and loving relationships. But we can hardly do that if everything is "throw away." Pretty soon we think of religion like that. We want it to be there when we have a "Big Mac attack" and don't expect to invest any time or thought or effort in it. But that's not the way God is. A living God means a "living" relationship—and one that is based on truth, not on some slick ad or quick thrill.

God as "Father"

We have seen that the God of the Bible stands against "idols." God is not an extra large human being. But in order to explain what the relationship with God is like, we have to use images that are familiar to us in our world. We are to think about God as like these familiar types of person or familiar human characteristics such as anger, love, mercy. At the same time, God is also different. God does not have our human weaknesses and imperfections. God is much more than we can conceive.

Images of Yahweh

In the pagan religions of biblical times, a god might be a father just like a human father. The god would have children with a goddess wife. But when Israel learned to speak of her God as "father," she knew that Yahweh did not have a wife and divine children. Instead, Yahweh's "offspring" had to be the people God had chosen. God had rescued them from slavery in Egypt in the time of Moses, had given them a law to live by, had seen them established in their own land, and had promised to remain with them if they would be faithful to God.

But, the Old Testament tells us, Israel did not live as God had instructed her. She kept trying to be like the other nations around her. Instead of creating a society which cared about all its members, even the weakest, the widows and orphans, the people allowed the rich to gain their wealth by injustice. They cheated people in business. They didn't pay on time the wages of people who worked in their fields. The courts and judges were corrupt and favored the rich over the poor. They even seem to have mixed pagan rituals and practices with the worship of Yahweh. And, perhaps worst of all, they thought that as long as they kept on making rich offerings and sacrifices to God, God would protect them.

God sent the people prophets to call them back to the law which they had promised to uphold. The prophets reminded the people that they owed everything to God. They pointed out that God's law called for justice and goodness. And they warned the people that if they continued to live as they were, God would punish them. The foreign powers would conquer the small kingdoms of Israel and Judah. The people would have to go back into exile and slavery.

Of course, you might think that if the people were so disobedient, God should just get rid of them. God could choose a new nation, perhaps. That thought occurred to the prophets too. And that's when some of them began to speak of God as the "father" of the people. Or sometimes they pictured God as the husband of a faithless wife. The image of God as a parent makes us see that God cannot abandon the people. God can punish them, but God can't trade them in.

Children of God

That's the way things are in a human family, no matter how bad things are between children and their parents. Even if you run away or lose your parents, they are still your parents. There may be days when your parents think it would be nice if they could "trade you in" for some other child. And there are probably days when you would like to "trade in" your parents too. Maybe you like a friend's mother or father better than yours. But you can't do that no matter what. You may find other adults who help you out in ways that your parents can't sometimes. But you still are part of the family you were born into.

Well, that's what it's all about when the Bible starts to think about the relationship between God and the people as a "family." The prophet Hosea wrote a beautiful passage in which Yahweh speaks about Israel as a wayward son:

When Israel was a child, I loved him, and out of Egypt
I called my son.
The more I called them, the more they went from me;
they kept sacrificing to the Baals [= a god of the Ca-
naanite people around Israel] and burning incense to
idols.
Yet it was I who taught Ephraim to walk,
I took them up in my arms; but they did not know that
I healed them.
I led them with cords of compassion, with the bands of
love, and I became to them as one who eases the yoke
on their jaws, and I bent down to them and fed them.
(Hosea 11:1–4)

You can see that this image of Yahweh and Israel as parent and child plays on the irrationality of a child abandoning a loving parent. Israel thinks that the gods of the surrounding peoples, the

Baals, which were associated with the fertility of the land, will take care of her. Yet it is God who has taught and cared for the child. God has carried her burdens. Thus, the image of God as "father" emphasizes the unconditional love that God shows for the people.

A Loving Dad

Jesus taught his disciples to address God as "Father." He used a word in Aramaic (the language spoken by the semitic people living in Palestine), "Abba." This word is a striking one because it was also a word which could be used within the family by children. Its impact would be something like Jesus telling us to think of God as "Dad" or "Mom," even. It doesn't make God distant and far away. It makes God close to us. It makes God someone who cares.

St. Paul reminds the Christians that a special moment in their baptism occurred when they could call on God as "Abba" (Gal 4:6; Rom 8:15). Baptism makes the Christians the beloved children of God just like the people of Israel in the Old Testament. Most of Paul's converts had been pagans. Their gods and goddesses often had to be addressed with long prayers. These prayers required carefully worded titles like the ones you would use for a king or some other high official. Any mistake in addressing the god or goddess and your prayer wouldn't be answered. The god might even become angry and bring you "bad luck."

Jesus and the early Christians said that their God was just the opposite. When he teaches the disciples the Lord's Prayer, Jesus keeps it very simple. First, we honor God by asking that others will come to praise God's name and do God's will. Then we present our basic need for God. And we acknowledge that the love and mercy which God shows us, we have to show to other people. Finally we ask God to keep us safe from the various forces of evil.

God Knows All

The Gospel of Matthew puts the Lord's Prayer in a context which reminds us of two things about God: God is already concerned about our needs, and we can't expect God to just go on helping us without some change in the way we live:

And in praying do not heap up empty phrases as the pagans do, for they think that they will be answered because of all their words. Do not be like them because your Father knows what you need before you ask. Pray like this:

Our Father, who art in heaven,
Hallowed be Thy name.
Thy kingdom come,
Thy will be done, on earth as it is in heaven.
Give us this day our daily bread;
And forgive us our trespasses,
As we forgive those who trespass against us.
And lead us not into temptation, but deliver us from
    evil.

For if you forgive others their trespasses, your
heavenly Father also will forgive you; but if you do
not forgive others their trespasses, neither will your
Father forgive your trespasses (Mt 6:7–15).

The Forgiving Father

Forgiveness is one of the most important parts of Jesus' image of God. The Gospel calls upon all people to learn love and forgiveness toward each other. God's love for us is not just based on what we "earn" by "being good." God cares for us even when we seem to have given up on God. Jesus tries to get that point across in a story he tells about a man who had two sons. One son stayed home, did everything right, helped his father out with the farm. The younger son split for a big city where he lost all his money on various cheap pleasures and girls. Left in a strange city with no friends and no money, the only job he could get was to work minding the pigs for some non-Jew. But that man didn't even give him anything to eat and there was a famine in the country. So the younger son decides he'd be better off going home and taking his chances that maybe his father would give him a servant's job on his farm at least.

The Prodigal Son

Can you think of anything that would be similar to this story in your experience? What do you think your father or mother would do if you or one of your sisters or brothers came home like the younger son in Jesus' story? Here's what Jesus told his audience happened:

> And he [the younger son] got up and went to his father's. While he was still far off, his father saw him and had compassion and ran and hugged him and kissed him. The son said, "Father, I have sinned against heaven and before you. I am no longer worthy of being called your son." But the father said to his servants, "Quick. Bring the best clothes and put them on him, and put a ring on his hand and shoes on his feet; and get the fat calf and kill it and let's eat and celebrate, for my son here was dead and is alive again; was lost and is found" (Lk 15:20–24).

The Faithful Brother

Well, you haven't forgotten about the older brother, have you? He was out working in the fields at the time. When he got back near the house and heard all the noise, he got the servants to find out what was going on. When he found out what his father had done, he got mad and wouldn't go in. So his father went out looking for him and asked him what was wrong. What was wrong? Can you figure out why he was upset? This is what the older son said to the father:

> He answered his father, "For all these years I have served you and never disobeyed your orders; but you never even gave me a goat to celebrate with my friends. But when this son of yours comes, who spent all your money on women, you kill a fattened calf for him!" And the father said to him, "Son, you are always with me and everything I have is yours. It was right to celebrate and be happy, because your brother here was dead and is alive; was lost and is found" (Lk 15:29–32).

This story is meant to tell us what kind of parent God is. The father in the story loves both of his sons. He wants them both to be with him. The older boy feels that his father doesn't love him as much even though he has been good. The father rejects that idea. He does love the older boy and he does appreciate what the older one does. But there's also a place to rejoice and celebrate with the boy who has come home. That's what God really wants. God's not interested in seeing how many people deserve to be punished because they are bad. The God we believe in wants people to return like the son coming home, or to remain faithful like the son who never left. And he wants them to celebrate and rejoice together when someone does come home.

Almighty, Creator of Heaven and Earth

We started out with God as we know God best—God as the one who cares for us as human beings. But the picture of God in the Bible goes beyond that. God is the Creator, the one with power greater than anything in the whole universe. Probably you have seen pictures of bomb explosions on TV. That may be the most powerful thing you can imagine. To imagine God as "all powerful" (= almighty) means that God is even more powerful than that. One of the most frightening things people in Jesus' day could experience was a storm at sea. If you have ever been out in a small sailboat when a gale came up, you know that even today that's pretty scary. Jesus' disciples were terrified. Jesus wanted them to learn that they could have faith in God's power.

Jesus Calms the Storm

Here's a story of how Jesus stopped a storm at sea to teach the disciples that lesson. Notice something. The disciples accuse Jesus of not caring what happens to them. We might think that God is like that too. We don't always understand why bad things happen or why God doesn't show off the divine power more.

A big wind storm came up, and waves were banging against the boat so that it was already filling up with water. But Jesus was asleep on a cushion in the back of the boat. The disciples woke him up and said, "Teacher, don't you care if we die?" And he woke up and rebuked the wind and said to the sea, "Be calm!" And the wind stopped and there was a great calm. He said to them, "Why are you afraid? Don't you have any faith?" And

they were amazed and said to each other, "Who is this
that even the wind and sea obey him?" (Mk 4:37–41).

The answer to the question "Who is this?" can only be that
Jesus is acting with God's power. The reason that God is able to
control the wind and the sea is that God is the one who created
them in the first place. Most of the religions of the world have
stories about how the world came to be created. The Bible opens
up with two stories of God creating the world. The first one, Genesis 1:1—2:3, is organized around the days of the week. On the
sixth day, God creates humanity, men and women, and gives
them everything else that had been created on the earth. Then, on
the seventh day, God rests from creation. By doing that, God
gives humans an example. They are also supposed to "rest from
work" on the seventh day. And they are to give thanks to God for
everything God has given them.

The Creation of Adam and Eve

Right after this story, the Bible has another story about God
creating everything. It is probably older than the first story because God acts much more like a human being in this story. In it
God begins by creating Adam, then plants, rivers and animals.
But when God finds that none of those things make a good com-
panion for Adam, he makes "woman," Eve. She is a good com-
panion because, according to the story, she is made out of Adam
(Gen 2:4–24).

This second story also has a religious message. During the
process in which God creates the bountiful garden for humans to
live in, God gives a command. They are to leave one tree alone,
"the knowledge of good and evil." That doesn't seem like too
much to ask when you consider everything that they have been

given. But in the next chapter, Genesis 3, the serpent tricks them into eating with the promise that it will make them "like God." Of course, it doesn't. Instead, we see them worried about not having clothes, hiding from God, and trying to blame the other person or the serpent for what they have done. Pretty classic "guilty" reactions. Maybe you've even done some of the same things when your parents caught you doing something you shouldn't.

The Fall

Well, God does punish all three, Adam, Eve and the serpent. They don't get to live a life free from work, pain and death in the garden anymore. So this very old story taught people that they should be faithful to God's command. It explained the origins of the evils of human life and of the created world as the result of an original failure to obey God. And it shows how human beings try to hide from their responsibility and shift the blame on to someone or something else.

That way of acting will get us into trouble every time. There's also another part to the story. The serpent is able to "get Eve" to disobey by telling her that God is really keeping something from her. She won't get hurt if she eats from that tree. It'll really be something good that God doesn't want her to have because then she'll be too much like God. Of course, the serpent is the liar. But by the time Eve and Adam find that out it is too late.

I bet if you think about it, you can think of some times when you've "been had" by an argument like the serpent's. "It really won't hurt you," or "Your parents (teachers) are just putting you on," or "Try it, you'll like it." And maybe you even gave in to the pressure. But was it really what you were promised? Even if no one "found out," do you really think it was right for someone to use that kind of pressure on you?

Caring for God's Creation

There is another side to the message that God created everything. God creates the garden and the earth and the animals for human beings. But human beings are also supposed to be responsible for that creation. Being "in charge" of the earth that God has given us means that we have to be concerned about it. It doesn't mean that we can just do anything we want. The first creation story in Genesis emphasized the fact that creation is "good."

It's our job to see that creation keeps that goodness. We are not free to destroy nature or the earth. If we do that, then we will have to answer to God, not just to some human committee or other. The second creation story paints a picture of Adam's relationship with animal life through the process of naming. How do animals in your life get named? We have a joke in our family that all birds are named "Timothy" or "Timmy." When my niece couldn't decide what to name her parakeet, my brother said to her (as a joke) that he knew a good name for a bird—that's right, her bird is now "Timmy" (along with a few other birds in the family). Well, it's important to name an animal, isn't it? When you name it, you set up a relationship with the animal. Now you have to take care of it.

Creation, the universe, is not just a vast collection of matter with which we can do anything we want. God is the power and meaning of everything that exists. Of course, we learn in school that the solar system, the planets, the earth and life on earth had to develop in a long process. Some types of animals that once existed, like dinosaurs, no longer do. The Bible's creation stories don't have information like that in them. They want to show us who is behind everything that ever has lived or ever will —God.

The creation stories also want to show us what our relationship with that creation is to be. We are not to destroy and ruin it.

We live with creation, discover new things about it and even make changes in it. But we also have to remember that the whole universe and everything living in it is a gift. We have to take care of that gift. God has made us responsible for something which is good.

2

Jesus: God's Son

and in Jesus Christ,
his only Son, our Lord,
who was conceived by the Holy Spirit,
born from the virgin Mary,

Jesus Christ

As soon as we mention the name "Jesus Christ," we have come to the heart of what makes Christianity different from other religions. We believe that the salvation of the world is linked to a very special human being. The name "Jesus" is a Greek translation of the Aramaic name "Jesuha" or Josuha. It was a popular name among the Jewish people. Matthew's Gospel gives an explanation for why Joseph was to give the child that name:

You will call him "Jesus," because he will save his people from their sins (Mt 1:21).

What's in a Name?

The name "Jesus" or "Jesuha" means "Yahweh saves." That is why the name had been popular among Jews. It reminded them that God was the one who saved them from slavery in Egypt and from the other dangers they had faced in their long history.

Maybe your parents had a special reason for giving you the name they did. Have you ever asked what your name means? People in ancient times took names very seriously. If you were named after a relative or an ancestor, you were to be like that person.

Jesus got his name "from God," since an angel told Joseph in a dream that the child should be named "Jesuha." This name reminded people of what God had done for them in the past. It also predicted what Jesus would do for us: save us from sin. Joseph must have wondered what was in store for this small baby when he gave him that name.

Christ—The Anointed One

We often attach another word to Jesus, "Christ." That word is not really a "last name." People who needed to distinguish Jesus from other people would have either added a reference to his adoptive father, Joseph, and said "Jesus, son of Joseph," or they would have referred to his village, "Jesus of Nazareth." "Christ" is another Greek word that was used to translate the Aramaic word "messiah" which means "anointed." "Jesus Christ" means "Jesus, the anointed."

In ancient times, kings and priests were anointed when they took their office. The Old Testament told stories about God sending a prophet to anoint people chosen to lead Israel. Even today anointing is part of the ceremony installing a king or queen or part of the ceremonies for a new priest. The "anointed" person has a special role in leading and representing the community before God.

At the time of Jesus, "messiah" would have meant a person sent by God as the king in the line of David or as a political savior of the people. Many Jews were hoping that God would send them a person like that to get rid of the Romans and to restore the nation to the glory it had had in the time of King David and his son Solomon. Jesus didn't turn out to be that kind of political savior. When Pilate had him crucified, he told the guards to list Jesus' crime as "king of the Jews." Pilate had Jesus killed because he thought Jesus was trying to get the people to revolt against the Romans.

Even though Jesus was not a king or political leader of the people, the Christians insisted that he was "messiah." Jesus was the person God sent to save the people. But Jesus did not come to liberate them from the Romans. Jesus came to save them from the powers of sin and death. Those are the powers which lie behind every kind of persecution and injustice.

Jesus' Temptations in the Wilderness

The Gospels tell a story about the beginning of Jesus' ministry (Mt 4:1–11; Lk 4:1–13). After Jesus had been baptized, he went into the desert to fast and pray. Jesus had to discover what it was that God was asking of him. During that time, he was tempted by Satan. The temptation was to become a powerful, political messiah. We remember the time Jesus spent in the wilderness during the forty days of Lent every year.

If you saw the movie "Vision Quest," you can understand how important the story about Jesus in the wilderness is. The name of the movie is taken from an indian custom. A young man would have to go out into the woods alone on a "vision quest." Different tribes had different customs. In some tribes, you would have to meet up with the animal that would be your guardian spirit or protector. In others, the visions you saw or dreams you had during that time would indicate your place in the tribe as an adult.

Jewish boys in Jesus' time did not have to do anything like that. But other people who felt God calling them in special ways might go to deserted places and fast and pray for a special revelation from God. They were following a pattern set by the prophets like Elijah long ago. The stories which the Gospels tell us about Jesus' "vision quest" are meant to show us the understanding of himself and his mission from God that Jesus had.

Jesus Rejects the Devil's Temptations

Jesus rejects all the temptations to worldly power. He could have had the whole world at his feet. But to do that he would have had to abandon God and serve "Satan." The devil is very clever. He even quotes passages from the Bible in which God promises to protect people to tempt Jesus to use divine power to gain himself glory and honor. But every time, Jesus has an answer. The devil tries to get Jesus to overcome hunger by turning stones into bread. Jesus answers that living by bread isn't enough. Then the devil promises to give Jesus all the nations of the world in return for Jesus' worshiping him. Jesus answers by insisting that the only one we are to worship is God. Finally, the devil shows Jesus the whole city of Jerusalem spread out below. He challenges Jesus to jump off the high tower of the temple. God will protect him. Jesus answers that a person should not put God to the test in that way.

Jesus' View of Power

These dramatic episodes show us that Jesus does not look at power and glory the way other people might. It's not enough for human beings to have all the material things they want. It's not right to attain all the nations of the world (as the Romans had done in their great empire) if one has to give up worshiping God to do it. And even someone with the miraculous power Jesus has recognizes that those powers come from God. He can't take them for granted or "put God to the test" with the kind of display the devil was suggesting.

Thus, we have learned already that Jesus will not be the kind of political messiah people expect. Later in the Gospels we see that even Jesus' own disciples have a hard time understanding that in order to really save the people, Jesus, "the messiah," will die on the cross. He will not lead them to be a glorious new nation or give them an empire like that of the Romans.

His Only Son, Our Lord

Jesus did not fulfill the expectations that many people had for the "messiah," the "christ." Yet, Christians believe that Jesus did bring God's salvation to the world. And he did so in a special way. Jesus was more than a great religious thinker, a great prophet or a great political leader. When Christians speak of Jesus as the "only Son" of God, they are claiming that a special relationship existed between Jesus and God.

Like "anointed," the phrase "son of God" would have meant many things to people in the time of Jesus. It was often used for rulers. The Egyptian pharaohs were called "sons of god" because it was thought that the sun-god, Re, was the father of the pharaoh. A king or ruler might be honored by being called "son of the gods" or "son of god." Mythical heroes of the past were also thought to have been offspring of gods and goddesses. And sometimes people who were thought to have special divine powers for healing or who were famous historical persons were considered "divine men."

If we look in the Old Testament, we find "son(s) of God" used in a number of ways. Sometimes it means angels (Gen 6:2; Job 1:6; Ps 29:1). Sometimes, as we learned in the last chapter, it referred to the people of Israel in a collective sense (Ex 4:22). Israel is even spoken of in a special way as Yahweh's "first born son" (Dt 14:1; Hos 11:1; Is 1:2; Wis 18:13). In keeping with the use of "son of God" for the king, we find that the psalms spoke of the king as God's son (Ps 2:7; 89:27). A recently discovered Aramaic fragment from the time of Jesus speaks of a future king of Israel as "son of God" and "son of the Most High," phrases that we find applied to Jesus in Lk 1:32, 35.

It was also possible to speak of a particular kind of person as "son of God." That person was someone who was unusual for holiness or righteousness (Sir 4:10; Wis 2:18). The story of the righteous person as "son of God" in Wisdom 2 and 5 was important for early Christians. It helped show the meaning of what had happened to Jesus.

Success at All Costs?

The story starts out with the reasoning of people who do not believe that there is anything but this life. They have decided that human beings are just collections of matter which dissolve with death. And, they think, it is not even worth leaving a good reputation behind you because that too will pass away. Therefore, they conclude that the best thing to do with your life is to enjoy material pleasures and to get as much as possible. It doesn't matter how you achieve your success. Use whatever power you have even if you hurt the poor, the widows and the elderly (Wis 2:1–11).

But people like that can't stand the existence of the righteous. Even though they claim that nothing matters but this life and its power, they feel condemned by the good person. So they decide to insult, torture and even kill the righteous person. They say that if the righteous person is "God's son" then God can protect that person (Wis 2:12–20). Although they may think they have succeeded in proving that obedience to God "does you no good" when they kill the righteous person, such people are deluded.

A Special Destiny "with God"

The author of Wisdom insists that the righteous people have a special destiny "with God." Wisdom 5:1–13 has another dramatic scene. The righteous person is standing in the presence of God. When the evil people see the righteous one there, they begin to confess their foolishness. Everything that they had built their life on is no good to them. Their wealth, their pride, their persecution of others have, in the end, gotten them nothing. But the righteous person lives forever with God.

You can see how this story fits into the story of Jesus. People thought that they had finished off his claims about God when they crucified him. Even Jesus' own disciples had been frightened and ran away. But the Christians know that Jesus was not "finished off." Jesus lives with God. Some of our oldest examples of creeds found in the New Testament even speak of Jesus as made "Son of God" by his resurrection and exaltation to God's presence. Paul, for example, combines sonship, resurrection and the Holy Spirit in Romans 1:3–4:

> . . . the gospel concerning his Son, who was descended from David according to the flesh and designated Son of God in power according to the Spirit of holiness by his resurrection from the dead.

This same way of speaking is reflected in the sermon in Acts 13:30–35. The "good news" is that the mistake of the Jewish leaders in handing over Jesus for death has been reversed by God. God has raised Jesus and in doing so has declared that Jesus is "his Son." Acts 13:33 quotes the royal psalm in which the king is declared to be God's adopted son at his enthronement, "You are my son. Today I have begotten you." And forgiveness of sins is proclaimed in the name of this Jesus, who is "Son of God."

Jesus' Obedience to the Father

Of course, you've already figured out from the Wisdom story that in order for Jesus to be exalted as "Son of God" at the resurrection, he must have lived a life that showed a special relationship to God. You could say that the resurrection was an affirmation of what Jesus was already in his lifetime. One way in which we see that Jesus is "Son of God" in his lifetime is in Jesus' obedience to the will of God. This obedience is evident in the temptation story. Luke 4:3 and 4:9 have the devil challenge Jesus with the expression, "If you are the Son of God . . . " Jesus shows that he is "Son of God" by rejecting the temptations put before him.

As "Son of God" Jesus accomplished what God asked of him. An important turning point in Jesus' life was his baptism by John the Baptist. The Gospels do not describe Jesus' life prior to that time. We can only presume that he led the life of any other young man in a small village like Nazareth, living at home and pursuing the trade of carpenter that he learned from Joseph. He would have attended the local synagogue on the sabbath, where he would also have learned to read and write, and made the journeys to Jerusalem with his family and others from his village for the three great pilgrimage feasts: Passover, Pentecost and Tabernacles.

All that changes when Jesus hears John the Baptist calling the people of Israel to repent. The Gospel stories tell us of an experience by which Jesus hears God's voice proclaim him "beloved Son" (Mk 4:11). The same story tells us that the Holy Spirit descends on Jesus. Thus, the reader of the Gospel knows from the beginning that Jesus is God's Son and will be carrying out his ministry with the power of God's Spirit. Mark tells the story of Jesus' baptism as a private experience. The divine voice speaks only to Jesus (the second person singular is used). The people who surrounded Jesus did not know what had happened. Jesus' ministry, his death and his resurrection would be the public evidence for the special relationship that he had with God.

Of course, as the early Christians became more and more aware of how special the relationship between Jesus and God was, they realized that being "Son of God" meant more than accepting the obeying God's will as an adult. They began to seek ways of speaking about a relationship between Jesus and God that had existed from the very beginning. In Luke 1:32, 35, the angel Gabriel proclaims that the child Mary is about to conceive will be "Son of God."

We have seen what it means for Jesus to be "Son of God" during his life. He is perfectly obedient to the will of God. We have also seen that confirmation of Jesus' life as the obedient and suffering servant of God is implied by Jesus' resurrection and exaltation. But there is more. Jesus' activity as "Son of God" is not finished as though he had graduated from school and received some kind of diploma or had trained for a race and won an Olympic medal.

Our Relationship with Jesus

As the unique Son of God, Jesus is "our Lord." There is a relationship between the Christian and Jesus exalted in heaven. In his letter to the church at Philippi, St. Paul quotes a very old hymn about Christ which ends with the whole universe praising him as Lord:

> Jesus Christ,
> though he was in the form of God,
> did not consider equality with God a thing to be grasped,
> but emptied himself, taking the form of a slave,
> being born in the likeness of humanity.
> And being found in human form he humbled himself
> and became obedient unto death,
> even death on a cross.
> Therefore, God has highly exalted him
> and bestowed on him the name which is above every name,
> that at the name of Jesus every knee should bow
> in heaven, and on earth and under the earth,
> and every tongue confess
> that Jesus Christ is Lord
> to the glory of God the Father (Phil 2:5–11).

This hymn is built on a pattern of humble obedience and divine exaltation. Jesus identified with the "worst" conditions of humanity: that of the person who is "slave" and that of the "crucified" person. Of course, Jesus himself was not in slavery. But crucifixion was thought to be the worst form of death sentence. It was suitable only for slaves and the most awful criminals. The hymn also makes it clear that we do not worship Jesus as Lord in the way that a pagan might worship a particular god as his "Lord" alongside other gods. What happens in the life of Jesus is all to the glory of the one God, the one who is "Father" to Jesus and to the Christians who sing this hymn.

The Divine Nature of Christ

What is added to our understanding of Jesus when we affirm that he is "Lord"? This hymn gives us one answer. Jesus is not just a person we admire and look to for guidance. Jesus is one to whom we pray, one whose power is felt throughout the universe. Of course, like many of the other titles used for Jesus, "Lord" had more than one meaning in the first century. It might be used simply as a title of respect or nobility and would not mean much more than "sir." It might also be used to address a pagan god (or its feminine equivalent used for a goddess).

But when the earliest Christians used the title "Lord," they were not thinking of the pagan gods or of emperors. They came from a Jewish tradition which used the Hebrew and Aramaic words "Lord" to refer to God. 1 Corinthians 16:22 preserves an ancient Christian prayer in Aramaic, "marana tha," "Our Lord, come!" This prayer speaks of the Christian longing for Christ's return at the judgment. It may have been used as part of the celebration of the Lord's Supper. Other passages in Paul suggest that the early prayers had the people call out "Jesus is Lord" (1 Cor 12:3; Rom 10:9).

Of course, the early Christians were careful to speak of Jesus' status as Lord as something given by God. They did not want people to think that there were really "two gods" worshiped by the Christians. That would bring Christianity back into paganism. But when Christians speak of Jesus as "Lord," they are speaking of him as having divine status. It would take many centuries for Christians to find a way of speaking about God as "one God," yet comprising three "persons," Father, Son and Spirit. The New Testament writers get along by distinguishing Jesus, the Lord, exalted at God's right hand, from "God," which is almost everywhere reserved for the Father. The perception that Jesus is also divine comes through in Thomas' confession in John 20:28. He acknowledges the risen Jesus as "my Lord and my God."

The Human Nature of Christ

But there is more to believing that Jesus is Lord. The one who is worshiped as above all is not some mythical or anonymous deity. It is an actual person, Jesus of Nazareth—someone who lived a human life among us, and, as the hymn insists, even died in the most painful and humiliating way possible for a human being. No wonder Thomas had doubts when he was told that Jesus had been raised! In addition, if we accept Jesus as "Lord," then we have to deny that status or power over our lives to anyone or anything else. By the end of the first century, the early Christians would run into trouble on that point. They would find suspicious Roman officials trying to get them to offer sacrifices to the emperor as "divine." They refused even if it meant death. They were not trying to get people to revolt against the Roman political order. But they had a point to make. No human power or political order can claim absolute status. It cannot set itself or its rulers up as "Lord" in place of Jesus.

Today there are still Christians in totalitarian countries who face that kind of challenge. If Jesus is Lord, then the state cannot stand in his place. It cannot be permitted to have the final say about human lives, values, even religion. But for many of us the question of who is the "Lord" we worship is more subtle. Is it a rock star? Is it wealth, power, success? What is it that has your loyalty and decides your values? What are you willing to make sacrifices for? Or even what is it that you really pray will come soon in the future? Are you really willing to say the prayers of the first Christians, "Jesus is Lord," and "Come, Lord Jesus"?

Conceived by the Holy Spirit, Born from the Virgin Mary

Down through the centuries, this section of the Creed has been hard for people to understand. Some people forget all about the Jewish break with paganism and just think that this is another tale of a "god" getting a woman pregnant and producing a semi-divine child. No Jewish reader would ever think that! Some modern people conclude that the Bible is just using a poetic way of speaking about Jesus' special relationship to God. They presume that either Joseph or someone else must have fathered Mary's baby.

Of course, it is true. The most important thing that this section of the Creed wants to tell us is that Jesus is a unique human being. He is really human, not some mythical figure. And yet he has a relationship to God different from that of any other human being because the Holy Spirit was responsible for his conception.

But the New Testament writers were not completely naive about reproduction. Matthew 1:18–19 says that when Joseph found out that his fiancée was pregnant, he decided to break off the engagement quietly. We are told that Joseph was an "upright" or "righteous" man. The law would have instructed him to break off such a marriage. On the other hand, he does not wish to expose her to the public disgrace of a trial or accusation of adultery. Presumably, he would have used some other grounds for breaking his engagement. The angel of the Lord comes to Joseph in a dream and reveals Jesus' special origin "from the Holy Spirit." Joseph's "uprightness" is further demonstrated by his obedience to the angel's command (Mt 1:23).

The New Testament authors clearly insist that Jesus' conception was an unusual act of God. But we have even less reason to demand that Jesus must have had a human father than people might have a few generations ago. Biologists experimenting with new technologies for reproduction predict that within a decade it will be possible to manipulate a human egg cell so that it will produce an embryo without genetic material from a "father." Of course, we are not asking "science" to explain Jesus' conception. But if we believe that God's creative power is active in the universe, then we have no reason to insist that Jesus' conception could not have come about without any human father.

Mary's "Yes" to God

Mary's status as "virgin" guarantees that God alone is responsible for Jesus' conception. In Luke 1:34 "How shall this be?" makes this point for the reader. But there is more to this episode. Mary exhibits her own devotion to God's will by immediately accepting the angel's announcement (1:38). When we remember Joseph's reaction in Matthew 1:18–19, we see that this was no easy request for a young girl of fourteen to sixteen. In the structure of Luke's Gospel, Mary's immediate "yes" to God's will is contrasted with an earlier story. John the Baptist was also an unexpected child because his parents had been unable to have children (1:5–10). But his father had questioned the angel and been struck dumb (1:19–22).

Mary's role in salvation is based on her "yes" to God's will. It is not based on her virginity, which is a statement about Jesus. Jesus is "Son of God" in a very special way. But Mary's "yes" makes her a model of the believer. She is blessed because through her cooperation God's plan of salvation can begin.

God Assumes Our Humanity

These brief phrases tell us that Jesus' birth was not an "accident." Nor was it something which God simply forced into human history. Mary's "yes" accepts the coming child with all the love and generosity of human parents and family. Paul makes this point in a different way in Galatians 4:4: "God sent his Son, born of a woman, born under the law." Like every other human being, Jesus is conceived, develops inside his mother's womb and is born. The role of the Holy Spirit in his conception does not make Jesus somehow "less human" than the rest of us. And, like every other human being, Jesus is born into a particular culture, "under the law." He is not "superman" dropped on earth from some distant planet. Jesus is a real man who grew up in a Jewish village in Galilee at the beginning of the first century.

In these few simple lines, we have the astounding truth to which the Christian faith keeps returning: God has taken on our humanity. God has become "part of us"—part of our story and our world. Mary's "yes" reminds us that salvation is a story of God's offer and human response. That response is receiving an act of divine love which would redeem the whole world. When Catholics honor Mary, they are thanking her for generously accepting the will of God.

3

Jesus Crucified

*suffered under Pontius Pilate,
was crucified, died and was buried,
descended to hell.*

Crucifixion in the Time of Jesus

The paper this morning carried a story about a man who had been executed in the electric chair after all appeals had run out and the Supreme Court had refused a stay of execution. But the number of people executed for their crimes each year remains quite small. Jesus died along with two other men. The others were accused of being "robbers," probably people who attacked travelers on the road. Jesus was accused of stirring up rebellion against Roman rule. That's what the charge "king of the Jews" attached to his cross (Mk 14:26) meant. Three executions—more than in a whole year in many states!

When people today ask for the death penalty, they usually

43

say that particularly violent criminals, those who have engaged in brutal murders, are the ones who deserve to die. In Jesus' time, people looked on crucifixion as the kind of death that a particularly bad person deserved. Slaves and hard core criminals were crucified. So were people suspected of plotting against Roman authority. A number of crucifixions took place in Judaea for that reason. Roman writers tell us that the victim was to be crucified in a public place so that others would be discouraged from committing the same crimes.

In the Gospels, we have a striking picture of the "public" crucifixion of Jesus. We are told that people who were passing by made fun of him and of his preaching. They thought that whatever Jesus had taught and whatever he had claimed to be was disproved by his shameful death on the cross.

And those who passed by made fun of him, wagging their heads, and saying, "Hah! You who were going to destroy the temple and rebuild it in three days, save yourself, and come down from the cross!" Also the chief priests mocked him with one another and the scribes, saying, "He saved others; he cannot save himself. Let the messiah, the king of Israel, come down from the cross now, that we may see it and believe." And those who were crucified with him also made fun of him (Mk 14:29–32).

That passage really captures the way people looked at crucifixion in Jesus' time. We are so used to seeing crucifixes and crosses as good religious symbols that we find it hard to read a passage like that. It's hard to imagine how Jesus, whom we worship as Savior and Lord, could have been treated like the worst kind of criminal. But the fact that Jesus, the one worshiped by Christians, was crucified by the Roman governor of Judaea, Pontius Pilate, is an historical fact. It was even known to Roman historians.

At the same time, it is also part of our Christian faith. We are not allowed to forget or to skip over the suffering and death that Jesus endured. We saw an early Christian hymn even celebrated that "slave" death, that humble obedience, as the prelude to Jesus' exaltation in heaven. We know that Christians believe Jesus' death to be an act of obedience and faithfulness to the will of God.

Jesus' Suffering Was Real

We may still forget how real that suffering is. Sometimes people think that Jesus' special relationship with God made him immune to the pain that an ordinary person would suffer. But the Gospel stories do not support that picture. They all insist on the reality of Jesus' suffering and death. The Creed tells us to look seriously at the crucified one and never forget what he suffered.

During wars and rebellions hundreds of people might be crucified in a single day. The Jewish people revolted against Rome in 66–70 A.D. In 70 A.D. Roman legions were surrounding the city. They would eventually storm the defending walls and the fortress guarding the temple. They burned and looted the temple, which was never again rebuilt. All you can see of it today is part of the western wall known to the Jewish people as the "wailing wall." It embodies all the centuries of captivity and oppression endured by the Jewish people. In order to break down the spirit of the Jews who were trying to defend Jerusalem, the Romans crucified as many as five hundred captured Jews a day where people inside the city could see them.

How Jesus Was Crucified

Jesus was not crucified in wartime but in a relatively peaceful period. In peacetime, the Roman governor could order a person crucified for any particularly vicious crime. Since Jesus was not a citizen of Rome, he had no right to appeal to any other court. The governor would hand the criminal over to the head of the execution squad. The victim would be severely beaten with leather thongs that had pieces of bone or lead in the ends. Then he would be forced to carry the horizontal beam of the cross through the city to the place of crucifixion. Sometimes the charge would be hung around his neck. The Gospels tell us that a passer-by was forced to carry Jesus' beam (Mk 14:21). Jesus may have been too weakened by the beating he received to carry it himself.

The arms could be tied to the cross beam, or nails could be driven in through the wrists (not through the palms as in crucifixes). Sometimes, in order to keep the victim from dying too soon, a small seat was halfway down to support part of the weight of the body. The seat was pointed and increased the pain of the victim. A cross might also have a foot support. Our one skeleton of a crucified man from Jesus' time had the feet almost parallel, legs next to each other, with a piece of wood and a single nail holding them against the cross. The man must have also been held up by a seat under the buttocks and the legs bent and sticking out from the cross. Ancient writers suggest that the Romans experimented with a number of positions to increase the torment of victims.

Death occurred through suffocation. The crucified person would have to pull himself up with his arms in order to breathe. At the beginning, a person might be able to hold himself up for thirty to sixty seconds. But soon the time would become even shorter. He would suffer muscle spasms and eventually the exhausted person would die. Stories are told of people who lived for two or three days before they finally died. One way of hastening the process was to break the legs of the victim. That is what had happened to the man whose skeleton we have found. John 19:32 reports that the soldiers did the same to the two men crucified with Jesus but that Jesus had already died so they didn't bother. Jewish law required burial before nightfall, so it may have been typical of crucifixions in Judaea to hasten death in that way.

How Jesus Came To Die

We have a pretty clear picture of what Jesus' death was like. You can also see that people in the first century would have been "turned off" by the idea that a crucified person was really the "Son of God." St. Paul wrote to the Corinthians that the crucifixion of Jesus was a paradox to any kind of human wisdom (1 Cor 1:18–25). You can't use the crucifixion to convince someone that he or she ought to worship Jesus. But Christians believe that there is a special "wisdom" of God. When we look at the cross, we see God's messiah taking on the worst possible human suffering out of love for us. St. Paul tried to express what the cross means when he wrote to the Romans:

> While we were still helpless, at the right time, Christ died for the ungodly. Why, someone would hardly die for a just person—though perhaps someone would be brave enough even to die for a good person. But God shows love for us because while we were still sinners Christ died for us (Rom 5:6–8).

The Real Cause of Jesus' Death

Paul doesn't tell us to blame Pilate. He doesn't tell us to blame the Jewish authorities who handed Jesus over to Pilate. Instead, he tells us that the real cause of Jesus' death was the sinfulness of humanity. We all share that sinfulness, injustice and separation from God. There was something about Jesus' life and words that challenged those around him. Remember the story of the righteous person. The evil people were threatened by that person's goodness and tried to wipe it out by mockery and death.

Our Creed does not contain anything about the teaching and ministry of Jesus. And the Gospels give various false charges and counter-charges. We cannot tell what was really in the mind of the people who decided to see Jesus executed. They certainly did not think that they were killing their "messiah." They certainly didn't realize that the death of Jesus would bring sinful humans back to God. Even the disciples were frightened and confused. Luke 24:20–21 has the disciples on the road to Emmaus tell the stranger (the risen Jesus) that they had been hoping that Jesus of Nazareth was going to redeem Israel but that he was crucified.

Why Suffering and Death?

Human beings have a hard time imagining that suffering can lead to salvation. And we certainly don't think that anyone with the divine power of Jesus would choose suffering and death. Paul says that maybe we would be willing to die for someone really good, but for sinners? The Gospels also suggest that Jesus tries to teach his disciples that service to others, suffering and even death was the way he had chosen. But the disciples, like people today, didn't understand. And they didn't want to listen to a message like that.

When Peter tried to talk Jesus out of the prediction that he would suffer and die, Jesus rebuked Peter, "Get behind me Satan! For you are not on God's side but on that of humans" (Mk 8:33). Jesus taught his disciples that they had to be willing to deny themselves and even to lose their own lives to follow him (Mk 8:34–38). He taught them that they must be like the lowly. They must serve others. They must be "non-persons," which is what children were in his time (Mk 9:33–37). But even while Jesus is teaching them these things, the disciples are trying to "be great." They want to see who's better or whom Jesus will reward more (Mk

9:34; 10:28–31, 35–40). Jesus keeps telling them that they have to follow his example and let God take care of the rewards.

One of the things that made people uncomfortable with Jesus was the way he challenged them. They thought they had things all worked out, and then he came along and insisted that God wanted real devotion. God didn't just want people to follow their religious rules about which foods they could eat when. He wanted people to change what was in their hearts. When the Pharisees were criticizing Jesus' disciples for not being strict about the rules for religious purity, Jesus said:

> Do you not see that whatever goes into a person from the outside cannot defile a person since it does not go into the heart but the stomach and from there passes on out. . . . What comes out of a person is what defiles a person. For out of a person's heart come evil thoughts, sexual immorality, theft, murder, adultery, coveting, wickedness, lying, lewdness, envy, slander, pride, foolishness. All these things defile a person (Mk 7:18–23).

Jesus challenged some of the interpretations of the will of God as expressed in the law. He said that they were really doing the opposite of what God intended. You can't get out of the obligation to take care of your parents by declaring that your money is "donated to the temple" (Mk 7:9–13). You can't make your devotion to the holiness of the sabbath an excuse to condemn Jesus for healing a person who is suffering (Mk 3:1–6). You can't say that just because the law permits all kinds of divorce, it is all right with God if marriages break up (10:2–9).

Following Jesus

And then there are stories in which Jesus challenges a good person to go even further. One of the saddest is the story of the rich young man. Here was a young Jewish man who had really been a good person all his life. He is attracted to Jesus' teaching. But he just can't answer the invitation to become one of Jesus' disciples:

> A man ran up and knelt before him and asked, "Good teacher, what must I do to inherit eternal life?" Jesus said to him, "Why do you call me good? No one is good except God alone. You know the commandments: "Do not kill. Do not commit adultery. Do not steal. Do not bear false witness. Do not defraud. Honor your father and mother." He said to him, "Teacher, I have done all these things since I was young." And Jesus, looking at him, loved him, and said, "You lack one thing. Go sell what you have and give to the poor and you will have treasure in heaven; and come, follow me." At that, his face fell and he went away sad; for he had many possessions (Mk 10:17–22).

That's one of the saddest stories in the Gospels. But maybe we are all more like that young person than we admit. There are lots of things that we don't want to "give up" even when we know we should. Maybe it's too scary to risk change. This story shows us that even with the love Jesus has for a person, the person still has to "go out on a limb" to follow Jesus.

The rich young man just left sad. But other people got angry at Jesus' teaching. They could accuse Jesus of stirring up political trouble. Really what Jesus was stirring up was trouble in their own hearts. So they tried to get rid of Jesus of Nazareth. And Jesus showed us that he meant what he taught about God's love, about service and suffering, about not retaliating against evil, and loving our enemies. Jesus took the condemnation, death and suffering on himself.

Was Buried

We know from the skeleton of a crucified man found in a tomb near Jerusalem that the families of victims were allowed to take the body for burial. Jesus died away from his home which was in Galilee. The Gospels report that his body was taken for burial by a pious Jew, Joseph of Arimathea. Mark 14:43 describes him as a person who was sincerely seeking the rule of God. All of the Gospel accounts emphasize the fact that Jesus really was dead. He wasn't in a coma or anything like that.

The Importance of a Burial

Jesus' male disciples had run away, and the women might not have been able to obtain the body or a tomb in which to place it. One of the worst things that could happen to a person in ancient times was to be "unburied" or to be buried among strangers, not by one's family or friends. Jesus was so alone and abandoned that he might have been left without anyone.

Instead, we find Joseph of Arimathea making a wonderful gesture of mercy and kindness to this controversial Galilean stranger. He doesn't look on Jesus as a person to be laughed at because he died on a cross. In a very human and simple way Joseph cares for the dead Jesus. He buys the burial garment, wraps the body and puts it in a tomb (Mk 15:45–46)—not much of a funeral. It certainly doesn't compare with the funerals of famous people, great religious and political leaders and the like. It's the simple funeral of the poor.

But it's something. It's a gesture of human kindness and love. When he died on the cross, Jesus experienced the worst torture and brutality that humans had devised. Now as he is buried, we see the other side. We see the importance of the simple gestures of humans caring for each other. When we bury our dead, we are not just getting rid of an inconvenient, left-over body. We are showing our love. We are showing that this person is still part of our human circle of caring. Thanks to Joseph, Jesus was not left out of that part of our human life. Sometimes Jesus had turned other people's funerals into celebrations. He had been able to restore life to the dead person (e.g., Mk 5:21–24, 35–43). But Jesus did not ''rise from death on the cross.'' Jesus rose from the tomb, from burial. Even in our death and burial, we go where Jesus has gone before us.

Descended to Hell

This theme is quite unexpected. We hardly think of Christ ''in hell.'' Nor do we find much explicit treatment of this topic in the New Testament. The references that we do find there have several ideas linked to them. In order to understand what this part of the Creed means, we have to see what it says about salvation.

What About Those Before Jesus?

Jesus' coming, death and resurrection occurred at a specific time and place in human history. It is not a mythic story that occurred before the world as we know it. But we believe that Jesus' life, obedient death and resurrection are the basis of salvation for humanity. They have brought humankind back into a loving and grace-filled relation with God. One question is obvious. What about those who lived before or who are "outside" Christ? Does Jesus have anything to do with their salvation?

Some scholars think that that was part of the understanding of Christ's preaching to the spirits that is described in 1 Peter 3:18–20. 1 Peter describes Christ preaching to some "spirits in prison." If human beings are meant, then it would appear to refer to those who lived at the time of Noah but were not saved from the flood, since they were evil and did not obey God:

> For Christ also died for sins once and for all, the righteous for the unrighteous, that he might bring us to God, being put to death in the flesh, but made alive in the spirit; in which he went and preached to the spirits in prison, who formerly did not obey, when God's patience waited in the days of Noah, during the building of the ark, in which a few, that is, eight persons were saved through water.

Later in the letter, 1 Peter reminds the readers that all persons will have to account for their lives before Christ when the judgment comes. Preaching the Gospel "to the dead" provides the foundation for calling them to judgment as well as the living:

> But they [pagans who abuse Christians for not sharing their evil ways] will give account to the one who is ready to judge the living and the dead. For this is why the Gospel was preached even to the dead, that though judged in the flesh like men, they might live in the spirit of God (1 Pet 4:5–6).

You can see that there are two sides to the message of salvation embracing the whole world. There is the side of salvation, calling people to be one with God. And there is the side of judgment, calling people responsible for their lives. They cannot "get off" by saying that they have never known Christ.

Other scholars have found another side to this passage from 1 Peter. They think that the "spirits" are not humans but the fallen angels. Legend had it that such angels had led the pre-flood generation into sin (Gen 6:1–5). Stories were told about the mysterious Enoch (Gen 5:24). Many of these stories included heavenly journeys on which Enoch saw the heavenly places where the evil angels were held as well as heavenly places for righteous people. Here is part of a story in which Enoch sees the fallen angels. Though he is sorry for them, Enoch can do nothing:

> And they [his heavenly guides] showed me prisoners under guard, in unlimited judgment. There I saw the condemned angels weeping. I asked my companions, "Why are they being tormented?" They answered, "They are the evil rebels against the Lord, who did not listen to the voice of the Lord but paid attention to their own will." And I felt sorry for them. The angels bowed down to me. They said, "Man of God, please pray to the Lord for us." I replied, "Who am I, a mere mortal, to pray for angels? Who knows where I am going or what will happen to me? Or who will pray for me?" (2 Enoch 7:1–5).

Christ's Triumph Over Sin and Death

According to this picture, Christ's mission among the spirits is a proclamation that he has triumphed over sin and death. All of the evils those angels had brought to humankind have been destroyed. A similar picture of Christ's triumph appears in Colossians 2:15. There Christ's death on the cross is described as disarming the hostile powers and winning a great victory. Ephesians 4:8–10 pictures the triumphant Christ ascending into heaven like a conquering emperor. He leads behind him a great crowd of captives. These images show us that there is a side to evil which is greater than human beings. When the Bible speaks of Satan, evil powers, "principalities," demons and the like, it refers to that reality. But the victorious Christ has conquered those powers.

Thus, 1 Peter suggests two sides to the belief "descended into hell." One is the power of Christ's salvation to get beyond the limits of time and history to reach all humanity. The second is the breaking apart of the cosmic, "larger than life" powers of evil. Both sides mean something very concrete for Christians. They mean that Christians do not have to live their lives as though they were still subject to such powers. They share in the victory of Christ by living in holiness.

Beyond the Grave

Finally, there is one more side to the belief that Christ "descended into hell." You need to remember that "hell" or "Hades" is not always a place just for bad people. Many times it is used for the realm of death. People who lived there were thought to live a "shadowy" existence, not one that was full of happiness or joy. In several places, the New Testament speaks of Christ sharing that kind of experience of death, of actually being "in the abyss."

Romans 10:6–7 asks who will descend into the abyss to bring Christ up. Acts 2:24 speaks of God freeing Jesus from the pangs of death at the resurrection. That is also the answer to the question from Romans. The power of God is what brings Christ up out of the abyss. Finally, Matthew 12:40 compares the three days and nights that Christ spent in the "heart of the earth" with the days Jonah spent in the whale. We have already seen that Jesus shares our human death and burial. These images make it even clearer that he really did not escape anything that is part of the human experience of death.

Today on TV they had a news clip about a new kind of coffin to get for people afraid of being buried alive. It is wired with an alarm button in case the person wakes up. A few years ago, driving through rural Tennesssee, some people showed me a grave with a TV tower on top. The man had arranged to be buried with a TV tuned to his favorite shows. (I don't know who paid the electric bill, and I guess all the shows were on one channel!)

We think things like that are pretty weird. Our Creed thinks they are too, but for a different reason. They are weird because they miss the main point of this part of the Creed. The presence of Jesus and the power of God stretch even into the grave. They don't stop when the doctor signs the death certificate. They don't even stop with the burial services. The words of St. Paul in Romans 8:38–39 express the significance of this part of our faith:

> For I am sure that neither death, nor life, nor angels, nor principalities, nor things present, nor things to come, nor powers, nor height, nor depth, nor anything else in all creation, will be able to separate us from the love of God in Christ Jesus our Lord.

4

Jesus: Risen and Exalted

On the third day, he rose again from the dead,
ascended into heaven,
sits at the right hand of God, the Father
   Almighty

Resurrection in the Time of Jesus

Every year at Easter time, we celebrate the news that God
raised Jesus from the dead. But, except in church, we don't hear
people talking about "resurrection." Jesus' suffering, death and
burial are very close to experiences we all know about. "Resurrection" is not.

Death in the Old Testament
It may be a surprise to you to learn that for a long time the
Jewish people did not have any belief that people might go onto

57

some form of life beyond death. For most of the Old Testament, death is "the end." People experienced death and its terrors in life when they felt themselves cut off from God's presence and surrounded by enemies.

As he was dying on the cross, Jesus spoke the words of a psalm which describes the suffering of a person in this condition—Psalm 22 (see Mk 15:34). By the end of that psalm, God steps in to rescue the sufferer. Here are some of the verses of the psalm. You will be able to find some of the themes from the psalm in the crucifixion story.

> My God, my God why have you forsaken me?
> Why are you so far from helping me, from the words of
>   my groaning?
>
> In you our parents trusted;
> they trusted and you delivered them.
> To you they cried and were saved;
> in you they trusted and were not disappointed.
> But I am a worm and no man,
> scorned by men and despised by the people.
> All who see me mock at me;
> they make faces at me, they wag their heads:
> "He entrusted his case to the Lord;
> let God deliver him, let God rescue him, for he delights in
>   God!"
>
> Be not far from me, for trouble is near and there is none to
>   help.
>
> I am poured out like water, and all my bones are out of
>   joint;
> my heart is like wax, it is melted within my chest.
> My strength is dried up like a potsherd,

and my tongue sticks to my jaws;
you lay me in the dust of death.
Yes, dogs are around me;
a crowd of evildoers encircles me;
they have pierced my hands and feet.
I can count all my bones—
they share and gloat over me;
they divide my clothes among them,
and for my raiment they cast lots.
But you, O Lord, be not far off!
O you, my help, hasten to my aid.

You who fear the Lord, praise him!
All you children of Jacob, glorify him,
and stand in awe of him, all you children of Israel.
For God has not despised or abhorred the affliction of the
    afflicted;
and God has not hid his face from him,
but has heard when he cried out!

All the ends of the earth shall remember and turn to the
    Lord;
and all the families of nations shall worship before him.
For dominion belongs to the Lord, and he rules over the
    nations.

This psalm expresses a confidence that God will take care of the person who is suffering at the hands of evil people. Jesus had tried to teach his disciples that suffering, not glory and honor, was going to be the fate that awaited him in Jerusalem (see Mk 10:43–45). But the Gospels tell us that the disciples ran away frightened when Jesus was arrested (Mk 14:50–52), and Peter even denied knowing Jesus (Mk 14:66–72). Jesus on the cross has no one to turn to but God.

The psalm, of course, speaks of God rescuing the sufferer "in this life." Mark suggests that when Jesus began to recite this psalm, some people thought that he was calling on the prophet Elijah to come from heaven and rescue him from the cross (Mk 15:36–37). That didn't happen.

About two hundred years before the death of Jesus, some Jews began to think that perhaps God "took care of" the good people who suffer and die trusting in the Lord in a different way. God does not necessarily rescue them from the evils they suffer in this life. But God provides a glorious, heavenly destiny for the faithful. This idea was particularly important in the middle of the second century B.C. The Jews were subject to a king, Antiochus IV, who tried to outlaw their religion. Eventually they would defeat the power of these rulers and restore the purity of their holy temple in Jerusalem. Jews celebrate the rededication of the temple every year at Hannukah. Hannukah falls shortly before Christians celebrate Christmas, so Christians think it is some sort of "Jewish version" of Christmas.

But before the evil rulers were defeated, many Jews were killed because they refused to obey commands to do things against their religion such as eat pork, sacrifice on a pagan altar or turn over the holy scrolls of the law to be destroyed. Some people began to wonder what God was doing all this time. God could not be ignoring the victims of such a persecution. So they came to the insight that God would give such victims a glorious return to life. God would also judge and condemn their persecutors.

"Resurrection" in the Old Testament

People liked to tell the stories of the martyrs. It helped them realize how important their religion was. In one of the stories, seven brothers are cruelly tortured while their mother looks on. Then the mother is also killed. Here is part of a speech that the mother gives to her sons. She is urging them to suffer bravely because God can "raise them up" again. When God does that they will be victorious over their persecutors:

> I do not know how you came into being in my womb.
> It was not I who gave you life and breath, nor I who set
> in order the elements within each one of you. Therefore,
> the Creator of the world who shaped the beginning of
> the human being and devised the origin of all things will
> in his mercy give life and breath back to you again,
> since you now forget yourselves for the sake of God's
> laws (2 Mac 7:23–24).

This passage gives you a good idea of what "resurrection" meant to Jews living in Jesus' time. God would use his creative power to restore to life those who had been faithful. This idea was often combined with the idea that God would also bring evil people, those responsible for suffering and persecution, to judgment. Even if they thought they could "get away with it," they would find out differently. The Book of Daniel in the Old Testament was written during this persecution. It refers to resurrection, punishment and rewards in these words:

> And many of those who sleep in the dust of the earth
> shall awake, some to everlasting life, and some to
> shame and everlasting contempt. And those who are
> wise shall shine like the brightness of the heavens; and
> those who turn many to righteousness like stars forever
> and ever (Dan 12:2–3).

You can see that Daniel does not really think of restoring the body of the person. Instead, Daniel thinks of a heavenly immortality like the stars. There is a special glory for people who have taught others to remain faithful to God.

Many Jews did not believe in resurrection. They made fun of it because it seemed to do the impossible; restore the body to life. Or they pointed out that it was not taught in the most important part of the Scriptures—the law. The Gospels contain a story of a debate between Jesus and the Sadducees, who did not believe in resurrection. They try to set up a case in which "resurrection" appears to be absurd so that they can trap Jesus. Here is the story:

> And the Sadducees came to him, who say that there is no resurrection; and they asked him a question, saying, "Teacher, Moses wrote for us that if a man's brother dies and leaves a wife, but leaves no child, the man must take the wife, and raise up children for his brother. There were seven brothers; the first took a wife, and when he died left no children; and the second took her, and died, leaving no children; and the third likewise; and the seven left no children. Last of all the woman also died. In the resurrection whose wife will she be? For the seven had her as a wife."
>
> Jesus said to them, "Is not this why you are wrong, that you know neither the scriptures nor the power of God? For when they rise from the dead, they neither marry nor are given in marriage but are like angels in heaven. And as for the dead being raised, have you not read in the book of Moses, in the passage about the bush, how God said to him, "I am the God of Abraham, and the God of Isaac, and the God of Jacob"? He is not God of the dead, but of the living. You are quite wrong" (Mk 12:18–27).

You can see from this story that Jesus does not think that resurrection will be like a person coming back from what we call a "near death experience" and walking around in the same body he or she had before. Just as Daniel talks about shining like stars,

Jesus talks about a new heavenly reality too, being like angels. You can also see that Jesus insists that God has the power to bring this about. Indeed, God's nature as "God of the living" makes it appropriate that those who are faithful to God will be confident that they will go on living with God.

Jesus Has Been Raised

Although Jesus was confident that God would help him, his followers were not. They ran away when Jesus was arrested. Some of them even headed back to Galilee. The story in Luke 24:13–27 gives a good idea of how those who had believed in Jesus felt. Two of Jesus' disciples are walking along outside Jerusalem. They meet a stranger (the risen Jesus) who wants to know what they are talking about. They are surprised that he hadn't heard the news about Jesus' crucifixion. Then they say to him:

> We had been hoping that he was the one to redeem Israel. Yes, and besides all this, it is now the third day since this happened. Besides, some of the women of our group amazed us. They were at his tomb early in the morning and did not find his body; and they came back saying that they had even seen a vision of angels who said that he was alive. Some of those who were with us went to the tomb, and found it just as the women had said. But they did not see him.

Was Jesus' Body Stolen?

These words sum up the rather complicated events surrounding Easter. You can tell that when the women and the disciples first found out that Jesus' tomb was empty they didn't know what had happened. There was a story on the news recently about some teenagers who went into a graveyard, broke into a tomb there, opened up the coffins, pulled skeletons up to the surface and scattered beer cans around. One man who was interviewed was both enraged and amazed. He couldn't see how anyone would be so crass as to violate the most sacred burial place, a family tomb. Well, that's what the disciples thought might have happened at first. In John 20:15 Mary Magdalene meets the risen Jesus in the vicinity of the tomb. She thinks that maybe he works at the cemetery and has taken the body away.

Most of the stories of the finding of the tomb in the Gospels include a vision of angel messengers who tell the women what has happened. But they didn't know what to think of that message either. Mark 16:8 reports that the women were so scared that they ran away and didn't tell anyone. You must be wondering why Jesus' disciples didn't believe in the resurrection right away.

Restoration to Life

The answer is really pretty easy. Jews who believed in resurrection also thought that when God raised the dead for everlasting life or for punishment, God would bring the world to an end. The great judgment would occur. The earth would be recreated, and the righteous people would live in the presence of God forever. When Jesus restores his friend Lazarus to life as a sign that he will be restored to life, Lazarus' sister Martha tells Jesus that she knows her brother will be brought back to life at the judgment (Jn 11:24). She was probably a little annoyed at Jesus for even asking her that. But what Jesus goes on to tell her is that he is "the resurrection and the life," and that whoever believes in him, "though that person die, he shall live; whoever lives and believes in me shall never die" (Jn 11:25b–26). Martha is smart enough to know that what Jesus is telling her means that he must be the messiah and Son of God (Jn 11:27).

Jesus' Appearances After the Resurrection

But our earliest testimony about resurrection says that what finally convinced Jesus' followers were appearances of the Lord. The idea that Jesus was raised to life after he had been dead and buried was too amazing for them to comprehend in any other way. St. Paul is the only person who writes about having seen the Lord from first-hand experience. The stories in the Gospels come from later generations of Christians who had heard them handed down from the first generation. In 1 Corinthians 15:3–11, Paul describes the basic beliefs of the Church and then adds a list of witnesses to the resurrection:

> For I delivered to you as of first importance what I also received, that Jesus Christ died for our sins in accordance with the Scriptures, that he was buried, that he was raised on the third day in accordance with the Scriptures, and that he appeared to Cephas [Peter], then to the twelve. Then he appeared to more than five hundred fellow Christians at once, most of whom are still alive, though some have died. Then he appeared to James, then to all the apostles. Last of all, as to one born at the wrong time, he appeared also to me. For I am the least of the apostles, unfit to be called an apostle, because I persecuted the Church of God. But by the grace of God, I am what I am, and God's grace to me was not in vain. On the contrary, I worked harder than any of them, though it was not I but the grace of God in me. Whether it was I or they, then, so we preach and so you believed.

Paul's Witness

Paul's case is a good one to remember. Sometimes people think that just because the disciples missed Jesus so much and wanted to believe that he was alive, they came to believe he was. But that argument won't work with Paul. Paul persecuted the Christians. He didn't think that they or the teaching of Jesus was right. He didn't want Jesus to be resurrected, to be alive with God. In fact, he had probably made fun of Christians for preaching that. As a well-educated Pharisee, Paul would have believed in resurrection on the day of judgment. All he had to do was to point to the fact that the judgment hadn't come when he wanted to cut down Christianity.

But when Paul "saw the Lord," then he couldn't deny it. If God had done something so remarkable as to raise Jesus up from the dead, everything the Christians had been saying must be right. In fact, Paul not only became a believing Christian. He became an apostle like the others. He started going around preaching the faith that he had been trying to destroy.

Paul's example shows us that the resurrection of Jesus was linked to a number of important changes in Jesus' disciples. Not only did they lose their sadness and fear, they also found the power to go out and tell other people about Jesus. James, who had not even believed in his famous relative, Jesus, while Jesus was alive became the leader of the Church in Jerusalem. Later James would suffer a martyr's death in Jerusalem. Peter and the rest of those who had been followers of Jesus would also begin to preach about Jesus. Most of them, as well as Paul, will have died as martyrs within the ten years following the writing of 1 Corinthians. That is a pretty big change for people who were scared, who ran away, and who even tried to deny knowing Jesus.

Jesus Enthroned in Heaven

Remember, we saw that resurrection was something new. It wasn't just returning to this earthly life. One of the ways that the Creed shows us that difference is to speak of Jesus living in a special reality. Jesus lives "in heaven," at the right hand of God. Paul doesn't tell us much about his vision of the risen Lord, but the way he describes it makes it pretty clear that he is thinking of a vision which takes place from heaven. It is a revelation "from God." The stories which Luke tells about Paul's vision in Acts are very clear about this point. Paul sees a light flashing from heaven and Jesus speaks to him from there (Acts 9:3–6).

Believing Without Seeing

Most of us think of Jesus going up into heaven at the ascension. Actually, "in between" resurrection appearances, Jesus was always thought to be "in heaven" with God. But there was a time when the experiences of seeing the Lord came to an end. Remember, Paul spoke about himself being "last of all." The Gospel of John tells a story about Jesus' appearing to Thomas to dispel his doubts. But the story ends with a special blessing on all those people in the future who will believe without seeing the risen Lord (Jn 20:29). That blessing includes us.

Roman Belief in the Afterlife

At the beginning of Acts, Luke tells the story of Jesus' going up into heaven as the end to the time of resurrection appearances. For the first century reader, this story would have been quite something. In the first century, the Romans said that their rulers ascended up into heaven as their bodies were being cremated during the funeral rites. They claimed that the emperors, whether they were good or bad, got to live with the gods and goddesses. The Romans would even build temples and offer sacrifices in honor of the divinized rulers. Of course, even some educated Romans made fun of this custom. The philosopher Seneca wrote a satire about the ceremonies divinizing Claudius (who was the emperor when 1 Corinthians was written). Claudius was retarded and often the butt of jokes. Seneca called his satire ''The Deification of a Pumpkin-head.''

Well, now you can see something else important about this part of the Creed. It means that no ruler or other human being can claim ''divine honors'' like that. Only Jesus, who is ascended and enthroned at the right hand of God, can be honored with our praise and worship. Not too long after Acts was written, Christians in Asia Minor would find out just how much this belief meant. People would start trying to make them offer sacrifices to the emperor. When they refused, they ran the danger of being killed. In order to run that risk, you really have to believe strongly in this part of the creed. Jesus, and Jesus alone, is enthroned at the right hand of God in heaven. Jesus, and Jesus alone, deserves our loyalty and worship. No one can make us believe in any other false gods, atheistic systems or anything else that would be like making a Roman emperor into a god.

The Beginning of the Church

You can see why Easter is the biggest feast of the Christian year. We see that Jesus' death was more than that of a martyr, even one which God regarded as a sacrifice for the sinfulness of humanity. Jesus' death has broken through the ''chains of death.'' Risen into the new dimensions of living, enthroned with God, Jesus continues to be present to the Church. Even though the resurrection appearances have stopped, the Christians know the power of the living and risen Lord. Jesus' followers had been frightened, confused and demoralized. The resurrection not only sharpened their faith, it also got them going on a new mission of preaching the Gospel. Thus, Easter is the beginning of the Church in two ways. First, the living fellowship of Christians with each other and with the Lord is established. Whatever happens in the future, it will never be shattered as it was on Good Friday. Second, the community receives its own mission to the world. The Gospel message is to be proclaimed to all people.

5

Jesus: Coming as Judge

thence he will come to judge
the living and the dead

God as Judge

Remember our treatment of Santa Claus? Many people think of judgment as a big record of everything they've ever done. They imagine that God will run down the record for each person and total up what that person gets as a result of his or her life. That idea contains something valuable. It does remind us of a need to know what our life as a whole amounts to. When you are young, that may not seem too important. After all most of your life is ahead of you. And, if you're like most people, you'll change a lot. What you want to be, your jobs, your friends, where you go to school, people you fall in love with, where you live, all these things will change. So will your ideas and maybe even some of your ways of acting. You may even be a little sick of people telling you that "when you grow up" you'll see things their way. Well, you might. Then again, you might not. You don't know and neither do they.

With so much of your life still vague and undetermined, it may seem hard to think of judgment on that life as a whole. It's a lot easier to think of it as though some adult, parent, teacher, or law enforcement officer were keeping track of all the little things you do. Perhaps you imagine them writing down all the mistakes and foul-ups. If you're like a lot of people, you may not even think that you "get credit for" the good things you do.

The Judgment of Israel

With this feeling about judgment, you may be surprised to find out that the Bible starts out with the idea that the people of Israel as a whole are judged. Gradually, distinctions came to be made between the "righteous" and the "evil" people within the nation. But even then judgment falls on us not because of every little thing we do but because our whole way of life puts us in one group or another.

The prophets in the Old Testament were sent by God to preach a message of judgment and condemnation against Israel. The people of God were supposed to live according to the standards of justice, mercy and goodness set down in the law, which God had given the people through Moses. That law protected the stranger, the slave, the weak, the orphan, and the poor. The rest of society had to care about those people. If their society was to be "at peace" in the biblical sense, it had to mirror the justice and righteousness and mercy of God.

What happened, not surprisingly, was that the rich gained their wealth unjustly. People began to twist the law. The poor were crushed even further. So, God sent the prophets to call the people to repent. God reminded them that without the justice demanded by the law, all of their religious rituals were meaningless. And God warned them that they would experience judgment if they did not change. That judgment would take the form of defeat by foreign nations and a return to the captivity and servitude from which God had delivered the people at the time of the exodus.

Israel's Call to Repentance

Here are some famous verses from the first chapter of the prophet Isaiah. The sickness and sinfulness of the nation will lead God to destroy her at the hands of enemies. Yet, God still loves the people and is calling them to repent.

Hear, O heavens, and give ear, O earth;
for the Lord has spoken:
"Children I have reared and brought up,
but they have rebelled against me."

Ah, sinful nation, a people full of iniquity,
offspring of evildoers, children who deal corruptly!
They have forsaken the Lord,
they have despised the Holy One of Israel,
they are completely estranged.

Your country lies desolate, your cities are burned with fire;
in your very presence aliens devour your land;
it is desolate, as overthrown by aliens.

What to me is the multitude of your sacrifices?
says the Lord.

I have had enough of burnt offerings of rams
and the fat of fed beasts;

When you appear before me,
who requires of you this trampling of my courts?
Bring no more vain offerings;
incense is an abomination to me.
New moon and sabbath and the calling of assemblies—
I cannot endure iniquity and solemn assembly.

When you spread forth your hands,
I will hide my eyes from you;
even though you make many prayers,
I will not listen;
your hands are full of blood.
Wash yourselves; make yourselves clean;
remove the evil of your doings from before my eyes;
cease to do evil,
Learn to do good; seek justice, correct oppression;
defend the fatherless, plead for the widow.
Come now, let us reason together,
says the Lord:
though your sins are like scarlet,
they shall be white as snow;
though they are red like crimson,
they shall become like wool.
If you are willing and obedient,
you shall eat the good of the land;
but if you refuse and rebel,
you shall be devoured by the sword;
for the mouth of the Lord has spoken.
How the faithful city has become a harlot,
she that was full of justice!
Righteousness used to lodge in her,
but now murderers.
Your silver has become dross,
your wine mixed with water.

Your princes are rebels and companions of thieves.
Every one loves a bribe and runs after gifts.
They do not defend the fatherless,
and the widow's cause does not come to them.

Zion shall be redeemed by justice,
and those in her who repent by righteousness.
But rebels and sinners shall be destroyed together,
and those who forsake the Lord shall be consumed.

Isaiah was right, Israel was eventually overrun by foreign nations. But people came to see that the cycle of prophetic warning, disaster, restoration to the land and renewal never really changed things. Besides, the horrors of war and subjugation fell on those who were the victims of the injustice of the leaders and wealthy people just as much as it did on the offenders. Often enough the person who was responsible for an evil situation did not even suffer for it.

God's Final Judgment

As a result, people began to think of a different kind of judgment by the Lord. More radical action was called for. They began to imagine that God would finally step in and end the world of good and evil, of divided nations, of powers as we know it. God would completely destroy the forces of evil and would call up all people in judgment. The "wicked" who seemed to have gotten away with it would finally be punished and the suffering righteous would enjoy a reward of eternal happiness with God.

In the last chapter, we saw that this idea of a judgment of all things was sometimes linked with the expectation of resurrection. But when people spoke about God's judgment, they were not announcing universal condemnation. Indeed, they had come to think that the "sinners" were really so locked up in their type of false reasoning that they couldn't hear a message of repentance. Most of the preaching about judgment in Jesus' time was meant to encourage the righteous. The arguments of the "wicked" that in the end all people die and how they live doesn't matter could be pretty persuasive. So people had to be encouraged not to "give up" on goodness and justice even when that seemed to bring no reward. Being faithful to God, good and just, might even result in being persecuted.

Warning To Resist Temptations

Here's an example from a book written shortly before the time of Jesus. The speaker is telling the righteous people that they should not give in to the temptations presented by the sinners:

> I swear to you that in heaven the angels will remember you for good before the glory of the Great One; and your names will be written before the glory of the Great One. Be hopeful because formerly you pined away through evil and toil. But now you will shine like the lights of heaven, and you shall be seen, and the windows of heaven opened for you; Your cry will be heard. Cry for judgment . . . be hopeful and do not abandon your hope . . . you are about to be rejoicing like the angels in heaven. You will not have to hide on the day of judgment, and you will not be found like the sinners; but the eternal judgment will be far away from you for all generations.
>
> Now fear not, righteous ones, when you see the sinners getting strong and flourishing; do not be partners with them, but keep far away from those who depend

on their own injustice; for you are to be partners with
the good-hearted people of heaven.

Now, you sinners, even if you say, ''All our sins
will not be investigated or written down,'' nevertheless,
all your sins are being written down every day. . . .
Light and darkness, night and day witness all your sins.
Do not become wicked in your hearts, or lie, or alter the
words of a just verdict, or utter falsehood against the
words of the Holy One (1 Enoch 104:1–9).

You can see from this example that the point of believing in God's
judgment is not really finding reasons to condemn people. The
Bible associates God's judgment with God's demand that human
beings make goodness and justice the basis of their dealings with
other people. The Bible and the author of passages like the one
just quoted realize that when people act in ways that are bad for
themselves or others, they usually have some way of making it
seem like they're right and the good people are just ''stupid.''
Maybe they think they won't get caught. Maybe they think that
nothing matters anyway except what they want at the time. Maybe
they say, ''Everyone does it.'' You can add your own examples
of the things people say.

If we believe that God is the final judge of human actions and
that God has insisted that justice, concern for the poor and oppressed, fairness, mercy, love, etc., are the way humans must act
toward one another, then we cannot go along with what people
say. We have to realize that what they say is a distorted picture of
how things are.

Jesus' Coming as Judge

The New Testament Christians knew that the one who would judge the world was Jesus. They looked forward to Jesus' coming in judgment. In one of his earliest letters, 1 Thessalonians, St. Paul describes what the new Christians did in turning to the Gospel:

> . . . our Gospel came to you not only in word, but also in power and in the Holy Spirit and with full conviction. . . . And you became imitators of us and of the Lord, for you received the Word in much affliction, with joy inspired by the Holy Spirit; so you became an example to all believers. . . . They report concerning us what a welcome we had among you, and *how you turned from idols to serve a living and true God, and to wait for his Son from heaven, whom he raised from the dead who delivers us from the wrath to come* (1 Thess 1:5–10).

You can see that Paul does not tell the Thessalonian Christians to be afraid of Christ coming in judgment. They don't have to fear God's wrath because they have turned away from evil lives and false gods. They have even suffered for believing in Christ, just as Paul did as a missionary and just as Jesus did himself.

"Come, Lord Jesus"

For faithful Christians, the coming of Jesus from heaven is a time of rejoicing. The sufferings and problems of following Jesus in an imperfect world will be ended. As Christians we are even taught to pray for the coming of Christ. That is when the "kingdom of God," the will of God, will be completely realized on earth. We are taught to pray for it in the Lord's Prayer: "Thy kingdom come; thy will be done on earth as it is in heaven." Even though most New Testament Christians spoke Greek, they preserved an old prayer in Aramaic, the language of Jesus, "Marana tha"—"Our Lord, come" (see 1 Cor 16:22).

This prayer for the coming of Jesus was probably part of the celebration of the Lord's Supper or the Eucharist. St. Paul says that the Eucharist remembers the death of the Lord until the Lord returns (1 Cor 11:26). When Jesus established the Eucharist, he also told his disciples that he would not eat that meal with them again until they celebrated it together in the kingdom of God (Mk 14:25).

False Claims Concerning the Return of Jesus

People today are often confused about judgment because they hear some Christians claiming that judgment is right around the corner. Often they tell you that the threat of a nuclear holocaust is really evidence of the means that God will use to judge the world. And, they say, if you join their church (and only their church), God or Jesus will come and snatch you away from the horrors of the end that is about to come on all the rest of humanity.

Well, they are right that faithful Christians have nothing to fear from God's judgment. Faithful Christians are looking forward to the return of Christ. They will be united with God and reunited with their loved ones. These people get their idea that they will be snatched away from the earth before the nuclear destruction from a passage about the return of Christ in 1 Thessalonians. The Christians there were sad and worried because some Christians had died before the coming of Jesus.

Restoration of the Christian Community

In this passage, Paul is telling us that the return of Jesus will restore the love and Christian community that now seems to be broken by death. He quotes a tradition about how the return of Jesus will be in order to reassure them:

> For since we believe that Jesus died and rose again, even so, through Jesus, God will bring with him those who have died. For this we tell you by the word of the Lord, that those of us who are alive at the coming of the Lord will not go before those who have died. For the Lord himself will descend from heaven with a cry of command, with the archangel's call, and with the sound of the trumpet of God. And the dead in Christ will rise first; then those of us who are alive will be caught up together with them in the clouds to meet the Lord in the air; and so we shall always be with the Lord (1 Thess 4:14–17).

You can see that the whole point is on restoring the community of faithful Christians. That's what the judgment will be for us just as Jesus himself spoke of eating the supper with his disciples once again. It doesn't have anything to do with promising Christians that they won't die in a nuclear attack. In fact, the Catholic bishops in the United States recently reminded all Christians that they have an obligation to work constantly for world peace and to seek ways to reduce the dangers of nuclear conflict. Even though we are confident that Christ's coming will be an event of salvation for faithful Christians, the Bible does not promise us a "quick escape" if human sinfulness reaches the point of destroying our whole planet.

When Will the Lord Return?

Another thing that Christians who threaten you with the coming judgment often neglect is the Bible's teaching that Christ will return when we do not expect him. No one can predict the timing of the end of the world. People keep trying to do that. They did it in Jesus' day as well as in ours. But Jesus himself taught the disciples that even he couldn't tell them when the end would be. He said, "About that day or hour, no one knows, not even the angels in heaven, nor the Son, but only the Father. Take care, watch and pray, for you do not know when the time will come" (Mk 13:32–33). St. Paul gives the same message to the Thessalonians (1 Thess 5:1–11). And, like Jesus, St. Paul reminds the Christians that they have to keep up a strong Christian life. But, he tells them, they have the real "armor" for the judgment: faith, love and hope (1 Thess 5:8). Armed with these fundamental Christian virtues, the Christians look forward to Christ's coming as the day of salvation (1 Thess 5:9).

Jesus Teaches Us About Judgment

We have already seen some of the things Jesus taught his disciples about his coming in judgment. They would never be able to calculate when the end would come, so they had to be careful that they were always following the Lord. But they should pray for and await the return of Jesus with joy. At that time, they would experience the reality of a happy celebration with the Lord.

Of course, the reason we are longing for the return of the Lord is that we do try to follow Jesus. And Jesus often taught his disciples what it would mean to be "judged" according to the standards of the kingdom of God. Every time we say the Lord's

Prayer, we repeat one of Jesus' most fundamental teachings: "Forgive us our trespasses as we forgive those who trespass against us."

Christian Love and Mercy

The most important standard in the teaching of Jesus is the love and mercy that we show to other people. This petition in the Lord's Prayer is underlined by several of the sayings of Jesus which follow it in the Sermon on the Mount:

> For if you forgive others their trespasses, your heavenly Father will also forgive you; but if you do not forgive others their trespasses, neither will your heavenly Father forgive you (Mt 6:14–15).

> Judge not that you be not judged. For with the judgment you pronounce you will be judged, and the measure you give will be the measure you get. You hypocrite, why do you see the speck in your brother's eye and not notice the log in your own? Or how can you say to your brother, "Let me take the speck out of your eye," when there is a log in your own? (Mt 7:1–4).

We are always making judgments about other people. Jesus warns us that those judgments can land us in trouble. If they show that we are unwilling to extend mercy and forgiveness to others, then God will not show mercy to us. Or, often enough, someone else could see that the things we complain about in other people are nothing compared to our own faults.

How Many Times Should We Forgive?

Jesus also taught his disciples about the kind of mercy and generosity that is expected of Christians in stories. One day Peter asked Jesus how many times we have to keep forgiving a person. He thought that seven was a good number, but Jesus answered "seventy times seven," which means as many times as it takes (Mt 18:21–22). Then he illustrated that point with a story about a king settling accounts with his servants. One man owed the king an incredible sum of money—more money, in fact, than Herod's whole kingdom took in during an entire year. You could think of it as something like the "national debt" in our country.

The man comes into the presence of the king and asks him to have patience and he will repay everything. Well, that seems pretty unlikely. What the king does is even more unlikely. He takes pity on the man and cancels the whole debt!

You would think that the servant would learn a lesson from that incident. Instead, Jesus says, he goes right out and threatens another man who owes him money. The second servant uses the same words the first servant had used. And, indeed, his request for time to pay is a lot more realistic. He only owes about three months' wages for a day laborer. But the first servant doesn't have any pity at all. He gets the debtor thrown into jail.

When the king finds out about it, he then punishes the first servant (Mt 18:23–35). That may satisfy our sense of outrage, but we need to remember that we are being warned. We have to show forgiveness. A warning about the judgment is placed at the end of the story: "So also my heavenly Father will do to every one of you, if you do not forgive your brother from your heart" (Mt 18:35).

How Should We Treat One Another?

Jesus also emphasized the fact that people had to show concern for the poor and oppressed if they expected to receive God's blessing in the judgment. For example, he told a story about a rich man who completely ignored the poor beggar lying at his doorway. The rich man lived in great luxury and had great feasts. The poor man was all covered with sores and the dogs came and licked them. But when the two men died, the poor man was taken away from his suffering into heaven. The rich man was in hell. However the rich man was so stupid that he didn't even seem to realize what he had done. He tried to get Abraham to send the poor beggar down with something for him to drink. When that didn't work, he tried to get Abraham to send the poor man to warn his five brothers before it was too late. But Abraham tells the rich man that his brothers will have to learn from what is written in the Bible. If they don't pay attention to that, no miracle is going to change them (Lk 16:19–31).

The Standard for Salvation

In another story, Jesus told about the judgment in terms of a shepherd sorting out sheep and goats. He said that all the nations of the world would be gathered together, and then they would be judged. What is going to be the standard for salvation? How they have treated the poor and the weak:

> Then the King will say to those on his right hand, "Come, blessed of my Father, inherit the kingdom prepared for you from the beginning of the world; for I was hungry and you gave me food, I was thirsty and you gave me drink, I was a stranger and you welcomed me, I was naked and you clothed me, I was sick and you visited me, I was in prison and you came to me." Then

the righteous will answer, "Lord, when did we see you hungry and feed you, or thirsty and give you drink? And when did we see you a stranger and welcome you, or naked and clothe you? And when did we see you sick or in prison and visit you?" And the King will answer them, "Truly, I say to you, as you did it to one of the least of these my brothers or sisters, you did it to me" (Mt 25:34–40).

You can see that this standard of judgment applies to everyone. Because Jesus identifies with the persons who are weak and needy, helping them is really service to God. No human being on earth is let off the hook. People will not be allowed to argue that they "didn't know" how they were supposed to treat others. In fact, the way Jesus tells the story even the "good people" aren't conscious of serving Jesus. But God looks at the goodness of what they have done for others. On the other side of the coin, some people might claim to be very religious and go to church a lot. However, Jesus warns his disciples that even the ability to work miracles won't bring salvation if a person doesn't live the life of love, mercy and service that Jesus teaches (see Mt 7:15–23).

Joyful Anticipation of Jesus' Return

When we say we believe that Jesus is coming as judge of all people, living and dead, we should remember that we are also agreeing to live as Jesus taught. The New Testament Christians were not afraid of judgment. They looked forward to Jesus' coming again. For people who are struggling to live out the teachings of Jesus in this world, the judgment is a time of rejoicing and salvation. The powers of sin and death are ended once and for all. The righteous are united with Jesus and God in celebration and joy.

Living the Life of Christ

You may also have noticed that Jesus is very realistic about human sinfulness. He doesn't think that everyone is "really good." His stories show us people who are not good. The rich man is not charitable to the poor beggar at his door even though he has enough to celebrate lavishly with his friends every day and to dress in the best clothes. The unforgiving servant doesn't learn to forgive others even though he has received an unprecedented demonstration of forgiveness, one that he could never have expected.

We have to ask ourselves whether we are really acting more like these types than like true followers of Jesus. Are we unwilling to share what we have and always trying to get more for ourselves? Do we expect people to be forgiving and kind to us and then turn around and act in the opposite way with other people? Are we missing out on Jesus' presence in the less fortunate people who need our help? Or perhaps we are like the rich man in another way. Perhaps we think that there's always time to do something about "being good" later. Right now we just want to have fun with our friends. Maybe "when we grow up" we'll think about how Jesus expects us to live. Well, if we have any of these attitudes, then we ought to think twice. Maybe we can't say that we believe in Jesus' return as judge with the hopeful joy that should be ours as Christians. If that's the case, the message of judgment is a call to us to think about changing things in our lives.

6

The Holy Spirit

I believe in the Holy Spirit

The Spirit of God

The "Holy Spirit" is probably one of the fuzziest concepts in the Creed. "Spirit" can mean everything from divine power to an intoxicating beverage. (Notice how Peter tells the crowds at Pentecost that he and the other disciples are not drunk in Acts 2:15.) We first meet the image of God's Spirit in the creation story of Genesis 1:2. The author pictures the Spirit of God hovering over the dark, chaotic waters. The Spirit is linked with the word which God speaks as light, order and life are brought into existence. This dramatic story gives us one element in the picture of "Spirit." The Spirit is creative power which God uses in shaping and ordering primordial chaos.

The "Breath of Life"

The second account of creation in Genesis 2:7 adds another dimension to the word "Spirit." It is linked with the "breath of life." In the first creation story, it was said that God made male and female humanity in the divine image (Gen 1:26). The second story, which is from an earlier time and is more concrete in the way it pictures God working to create everything, says that God breathed the breath of life into Adam after God had made him out of the clay. That "breath of life" is a gift of God's Spirit. We see that the Spirit provides the link between humans and God.

The Work of the Spirit in the Old Testament

The activity of God's Spirit is not limited to setting up the world. Biblical writers believed that it was the Spirit of God that kept the world going. God's Spirit is behind everything. But they especially saw the Spirit of God at work in human beings. God inspired the great exploits of folk heroes like Samson (Jgs 13—16) or early kings like Saul and David. God's Spirit was said to rest on the king when he was "anointed" with oil by the prophet as in the story about the prophet Samuel being sent by God to anoint Saul, the first king (1 Sam 10:1–8). God has chosen Saul to lead the people and to rescue them from the enemies surrounding them. As Saul is on his way to the altar to make a sacrifice to God after his anointing, he meets a group of prophets. The Spirit of God comes over the king and he prophesies too. The story-teller has Samuel tell the king that this will be a sign that God is with the king in his endeavors.

Of course, the Spirit of God also inspired the prophets of Israel. The most important activity of God's Spirit was to guide the people in the way that God wished them to live. The prophets often had to struggle with the kings to show them what God wanted at a particular time in their history.

Several hundred years before Jesus' time, Israel had suffered a series of defeats at the hands of the great military powers. The leading people had been taken away to Babylon by the Babylonians or had been forced to flee into Egypt. Even though the Persians who defeated the Babylonians let the Jews go back to the land God had given them, things were never the same. Alexander the Great came from Greece and took over the Persian empire. Then his successors were thrown out by the Romans, who ruled Palestine in Jesus' day.

Awaiting God's Promised King

People looked back to the days when Israel had been an independent nation under her own king, and they hoped for a time when God would send his Spirit on a new king. This new ideal king would restore the nation to what it had once been. In fact, he would go even further than that. He would make it a truly righteous and just place where people would live according to all the laws God had given them. Justice would prevail and there would be no more poor people, no more evil, no more weeping and mourning in the land.

The "Servant of the Lord's" Mission

Sometimes they spoke of this ideal leader as the "servant of the Lord." Here is a very famous description from Isaiah 42:1–4 of how the Spirit of God will inspire the Servant:

Behold my servant, whom I [God] uphold, my chosen one in whom my soul delights; I have put my Spirit upon him, and he will bring forth justice to the nations. He will not cry or raise his voice or make it heard in the street; he will not break a bruised reed; and he will not put out a dimly burning wick; he will faithfully bring forth justice. He will not fail or be discouraged until he has established justice in the earth; and the coastlands wait for his law.

Later in Isaiah 61:1–2, we hear the ideal servant of the Lord speaking in the first person about the mission that God had given him:

The Spirit of the Lord God is upon me because the Lord has anointed me to bring good tidings to the afflicted; he has sent me to heal the brokenhearted, to proclaim liberty to the captives, and the opening of prison to those who are bound, to proclaim the year of the Lord's favor, and the day of vengeance of our God, to comfort all who mourn.

When the ideal leader comes, all of Israel's enemies will be defeated by God. God's people, who have been suffering, will be freed. That freedom is presented as the "good news" which the servant brings to the nation.

The Foundation of Our Relationship with God

You can see from these examples that the idea of God as Spirit is a very rich symbol. It describes God as the basis for everything that exists. It presents human beings as having a special, unique relationship to God. It traces heroic exploits on behalf of the people, the acts of wise political leaders, and the teaching of the prophets all back to God's Spirit acting in human beings. The Spirit also refers to the future. The hopes for an "anointed" leader, a person filled with God's Spirit who can restore the nation to its former glory and establish justice and peace in the world, all these hopes are based on the belief that the "Spirit of God" can guide human beings and their affairs.

The Spirit in the Life of Jesus

Maybe you've already figured out that when Christians talk about Jesus as "the messiah" (the word "messiah" means "anointed"), they are saying that Jesus is the person in whom those hopes for an ideal "servant of God" were fulfilled. The special relationship that Jesus has with God is based on the Spirit. In fact, St. Paul even wrote to the Corinthians, "The Lord is the Spirit" (2 Cor 3:17).

The Promise of God's Spirit

The Gospel stories all tell us that the Spirit of God came upon Jesus in a special way. Luke 1:35 has the angel explain to Mary that the Spirit of God is responsible for Jesus' birth:

The Holy Spirit will come upon you, and the power of the Most High will overshadow you; therefore the child to be born will be called holy, the Son of God.

The Spirit at Jesus' Baptism

But the most important manifestation of the Spirit in Jesus' life comes later when he is grown up. We don't know much at all about Jesus' life as a child and young man. When the Gospels pick up Jesus' story, he has come to be baptized by John the Baptist. The Spirit of God comes on Jesus, and God's voice speaks of Jesus' special relationship to God. God's Spirit then drives Jesus out into the desert where he is tested. Mark's account of these events only occupies a few verses:

> And when he came up out of the water, immediately he saw the heavens opened and the Spirit descending on him like a dove; and a voice came from heaven, "You are my Son; with you I am well pleased." The Spirit immediately drove him out into the wilderness. And he was in the wilderness forty days, tempted by Satan; and he was with the wild beasts; and the angels ministered to him (Mk 1:10–13).

This account leaves us no doubt that the Spirit of God is behind the ministry of Jesus as it is told in the rest of the Gospel. The heavenly vision also makes it clear that the Spirit rests with Jesus in a way that is different from the way in which it inspires others like John the Baptist. Jesus' relationship to God is that of "Son."

The Spirit in Jesus' Preaching Ministry

In Matthew and Luke, the hopes of Isaiah 61:1–2 are part of the opening preaching in Jesus' ministry. Luke 4:14–30 says that after the testing in the wilderness, Jesus came into Galilee "in the power of the Spirit." He preaches a sermon in the synagogue at Nazareth. The words of Isaiah 61:1–2 are the text for the sermon. Jesus announces that those words are now being fulfilled. Not surprisingly, some of the people in the synagogue were skeptical. Jesus, the one they'd known all his life, was claiming that he would fulfill the dreams of centuries (Lk 4:22). In Matthew's Gospel, these promises also form the basis for Jesus' first sermon. They are behind the Beatitudes that open the Sermon on the Mount (Mt 5:3–10).

You can see from these passages that it is impossible to believe that Jesus is "Son of God" without also believing in the Holy Spirit. Jesus' special relationship to God and Jesus' teaching are both related to the fact that the Spirit of God rests on Jesus in a special way.

The Spirit in Jesus' Healing Ministry

There is one further part of Jesus' ministry that is related to the Spirit of God—Jesus' healings. All of the Gospels tell us that Jesus was well known for his power to heal the sick. In many stories, the healings are of a special type—exorcisms. Jesus is able to drive out the "demons" which have taken over someone's personality. In those stories, the healings are almost like a contest of strength between Jesus' power and that of the demon.

In Matthew's version of the healing of the Gadarene demoniacs (Mt 8:28–34), the demons even accuse Jesus of coming to torment them "too early." What they are referring to is the judgment when God would completely destroy the powers of evil. They don't think it is "fair" for Jesus to come and bother them in advance. Of course, that objection doesn't work. Jesus throws them out of the men anyway.

Remember the promises in Isaiah 42:1–4? Matthew 12:18–21 quotes that passage in connection with Jesus' ministry of healing. However, the quotation from the prophet is framed by two episodes in which Jesus' ministry is rejected. The Pharisees do not see that the promised Spirit of God is at work in Jesus. All they see when Jesus heals the paralyzed man is that Jesus breaks the law commanding that no work be done on the sabbath (Mt 12:9–14).

All they see in Jesus' ability to cast out demonic forces from people is that Jesus must have made some sort of "deal" with

Satan. (The Gospel reader knows from the temptation stories that Jesus did not make any such deals.) Jesus demolishes the logic of their argument. He tells them that if Satan is at war with his own forces, then Satan is not going to last much longer. Besides, what do the Pharisees say about other healers of whom they approve? Then Jesus makes it clear that his healings are done by the Spirit of God. They are a sign that the kingdom of God has come (Mt 12:24–28).

Jesus concludes this section with a number of warnings. Any kind of sin can be forgiven except speaking against the Spirit. By claiming that Jesus was operating with the power of Satan rather than that of God, Jesus' enemies rejected the very basis for any salvation, the presence and activity of the Holy Spirit.

The Spirit and the Resurrection of Jesus

The final manifestation of God's Spirit in Jesus' life is in the resurrection. Remember, the power of life was linked to the Spirit of God in the very beginning. When Jesus was restored to life by God on Easter, the early Christians saw that God's Spirit was at work there too (see Rom 1:3–4).

The Spirit in the Life of the Christian

The hopes which people had for the time of salvation were not limited to the coming of an anointed leader (messiah). Other prophecies in the Old Testament spoke of a time when God's Spirit would come upon all the people. Instead of being separated from God by sin, the people would experience the unity with God brought by the Spirit.

The Mission of the Disciples

The story of Pentecost told in Acts 2 describes how the Spirit came to Jesus' first disciples. This story is very dramatic. The Spirit appears like fire and the apostles begin to speak in different languages. Jews from all over the world, who were in Jerusalem for the feast, heard the Gospel being preached in their own language.

When Peter starts to explain what is happening, the first thing he does is point back to one of the Old Testament prophecies from Joel 2:28–32. God had promised to shed the Holy Spirit on all the people when the day of salvation came. Peter tells the crowd that that time has come.

Peter says that when God raised Jesus from the dead to heaven, God also gave Jesus the Holy Spirit to pour out on his followers (Acts 2:33). This is an important point. The Spirit comes to Christians through Jesus. Sometimes Jesus is spoken of as though he were the Spirit, since he is the one from whom we receive the Spirit.

Another story in the New Testament makes this point in a somewhat less dramatic way. In John's Gospel, Jesus appears to his disciples at a meal. He tells them that just as God sent him into the world, they are going to be sent out into the world. Then he breathes on them and they receive the Holy Spirit and the power to forgive sins (Jn 20:19–23).

Both stories link the Holy Spirit with the mission of Jesus' followers to preach to the world. God's Spirit always leads to activity in the name of God. It is not some private possession just given to people. Calling others to believe means calling them to a new life with God. They are to turn away from their old lives of sin. The disciples receive the power to forgive sin just as Jesus had done in some of his healings.

The Spirit's Activity in Baptism

For the first Christians, receiving forgiveness of sin was linked with receiving the Holy Spirit in baptism. When the people who heard Peter's sermon on Pentecost asked what they should do, he told them:

> Repent and be baptized, every one of you, in the name of Jesus Christ for the forgiveness of your sins; and you shall receive the gift of the Holy Spirit.

Cornelius Is Baptized

These first converts were Jews like Jesus and the disciples of Jesus. Later on in Acts the first Christians begin to find that it is not just Jews from all over the world who hear the message but non-Jews too. There is a story about how Peter came to baptize the household of a Roman centurion, Cornelius, in Acts 10. The Holy Spirit is very active in bringing Peter to Cornelius' house. God shows that God's will includes baptizing non-Jews when the Holy Spirit comes on Cornelius and the others as soon as they hear the Gospel message preached by Peter. Peter concludes that if God has already given these people the Spirit, then it must be all right to make them part of the Christian community by baptizing them (Acts 10:44–48).

The Universality of the Spirit's Power

Other examples of the link between baptism and receiving the Holy Spirit can be found in Paul's letters. Paul writes one letter to Christians in Galatia. They had been converted to Christianity like Cornelius without becoming Jews. But some of them were wondering if that was right. They seem to have thought that maybe they should adopt some Jewish practices.

Paul says "no." He reminds them that the apostles had met in Jerusalem and had agreed that some missionaries like Peter would preach to Jews. Others like Paul and his associates would preach to non-Jews. The non-Jews could join the Christian community without being converted to Judaism (Gal 2:1–10). Then Paul reminds them of their conversion to Christianity. They received the Spirit and other signs of God's activity among them when they believed and were baptized. Paul reminds them that they did not need to keep the Jewish law then:

> Let me ask you this: "Did you receive the Spirit by works of the law or by hearing with faith? Are you so foolish? Having begun with the Spirit, are you now ending with the flesh? Did you experience so many things in vain, if it really is in vain? Does he who supplies the Spirit to you and works miracles among you do so by works of the law or by hearing with faith? (Gal 3:2–5).

Paul goes on to speak about baptism as the point at which all people are adopted as "children of God" no matter what their origin, sex or social status:

> For in Christ Jesus you are all sons and daughters of God, through faith. For as many of you as were baptized into Christ have put on Christ. There is neither Jew nor Greek, there is neither slave nor free, there is neither male nor female; for you are all one in Christ Jesus (Gal 3:26–27).

One of the signs that the new Christians were the children of God was the coming of the Spirit into their hearts at baptism. The Spirit made it possible to call out the prayer to God as Father:

And because you are sons and daughters, God has sent
the Spirit of his Son into our hearts, crying, "Abba! Father!" (Gal 4:6).

The special, personal relationship of the Christian and God is
based on the Holy Spirit. The Holy Spirit which we receive in
baptism makes it possible for us to address God as "Abba," to
use the prayer of Jesus.

The Activity of the Spirit in Prayer

St. Paul comes back to this connection between the Holy
Spirit and prayer in a letter he wrote to Christians in Rome. He
writes of the Spirit of God living in the Christian and speaks of
the Spirit's prayer "Abba" as evidence that we are the children
of God and brothers and sisters of Christ:

When we cry, "Abba! Father!" it is the Spirit itself
bearing witness with our spirit that we are children of
God, and if children, then heirs, heirs of God and fellow
heirs with Christ provided we suffer with him in order
that we may also be glorified with him (Rom 8:16–17).

Then Paul goes on to say that the Spirit actually helps all Christians by offering prayers to God that come from depths of the
heart. Even when a person can't find the words to turn to express
what he or she wants to say to God, the Spirit is there to make the
prayer for us (Rom 8:26–27).

Sometimes people think that the only Christians who have
the Spirit are people who have special experiences and gifts of the
Spirit. If you ask them about prayer "in the Spirit," they would
say that it is when someone is speaking in tongues or when someone with the gift of healing people is praying over them. But you

can see that the New Testament does not limit the role of the Spirit in Christian life to those "special cases." Every baptized Christian has already received a share in the Spirit. Every Christian who calls out to God in prayer is praying "in the Spirit." The Spirit is even helping us when we are struggling with prayer and when we don't know what to say to God.

Life "According to the Spirit"

Of course, there are many other ways in which the Spirit is active in the lives of Christians. St. Paul reminded the Roman Christians that if we expect to share the glory of Christ, then we have to share the suffering of Christ. We have to lead a special kind of life now. In the same chapter of Romans, Paul speaks of people who live "according to the Spirit" and others who live "according to the flesh and all the passions that human beings have." To live "according to the flesh" means that you are really against God. You don't follow any of the teachings of the Bible. You just do whatever you happen to want to do at the time.

Of course, when people act like that they think that it's going to make them happy. But Paul says that the only thing that really makes a person happy is to live "according to the Spirit." A mind that is focused on the Spirit, he says, is "life and peace," whereas one that is focused on the flesh is "death" (Rom 8:5–8). All of the virtues of love, kindness, charity, humility, caring for others and the like are the work of the Spirit in us as Christians.

In the Letter to the Galatians, Paul gives examples of the two types of life. It is a contest of the flesh against the Spirit:

> But I say: walk by the Spirit and do not gratify the desires of the flesh. For the desires of the flesh are against the Spirit, and the desires of the Spirit are against the

flesh; for these are opposed to each other. . . . Now the
works of the flesh are plain: immorality, impurity, li-
centiousness, idolatry, sorcery, enmity, strife, jeal-
ousy, anger, selfishness, dissension, party spirit, envy,
drunkenness, carousing and the like. I warn you as I
warned you before: those who do such things will not
inherit the kingdom of God. But the fruit of the Spirit is
love, joy, peace, patience, kindness, goodness, faithfulness, gentleness, self-control; against such there is
no law. And those who belong to Christ Jesus have crucified the flesh with its passions and desires. If we live
by the Spirit, let us also walk by the Spirit. Let us have
no self-conceit, no provoking of one another, no envy
of one another (Gal 5:16–26).

You can see that the Spirit is basic to Christian life. Without the
Spirit, no one would live as God has called us to do. Without it,
no one would even be able to turn to God in prayer.

The Spirit in Christian Witnessing

There is one more side to the activity of the Spirit in the life
of the Christian, the side of public witnessing to the Gospel. Remember, when a prophet or king was anointed in the Old Testament, it meant that that person was about to take up a special role
in the public life of the people. That person would have to be a
spokesperson for God or would have to lead the nation. Remember also that when Jesus' disciples first received the Spirit, they
had a new public role too. They had to go out and preach the Gospel to others. And for the New Testament Christians just being a
Christian meant that people might turn against them or persecute
them. But they knew that when they had to face such situations,

the Holy Spirit would help them there too. They were told, "And when they bring you to trial and deliver you up, do not be anxious beforehand about what you are going to say; but say whatever is given to you in that hour, for it is not you who speak but the Holy Spirit" (Mk 13:11).

Well, most of us don't have to face getting haled into court just for being a Christian. Most of us may never even be made fun of or called dirty names because we are a Christian. But we have to bear witness to the Gospel too. We have to take public responsibility for what we believe. Unlike most of the first Christians who were already adults when they were baptized, many of us were infants or small children. Even in the laws of our country there is a difference between an adult and a child. A child is not held responsible in the same way that a grown-up is. In our Church, we have a similar situation. You received the Spirit when you were baptized as a child. But when you get to be old enough to be responsible for your faith, then you are anointed with oil and receive a special gift of the Spirit to help you with your new responsibility. Once you have been confirmed, you have to give public witness to your beliefs. You, and not your parents, are now responsible for what kind of Christian you are. That's why we challenge people in our confirmation programs by asking them to show in some way that they really do want to live as adult Christians, that they really do want to "walk in the Spirit."

The Holy Spirit: Foundation of Everything

Many Christians don't think much about how important the Holy Spirit is in our religion. But now you can see that it is the foundation of everything. God creates and works in the world through the Spirit. Christians receive the Spirit through the risen and exalted Jesus when they are baptized. The Spirit established a special closeness between us and God that we invoke whenever we pray, and especially when we pray the ancient prayer, "Abba." The Spirit also inspires and guides our Christian life so that we will eventually come to claim our inheritance of glory with Christ.

7

The Holy Catholic Church

the holy, catholic church,
the communion of saints,
the forgiveness of sins

The Church, Holy
and Catholic

It may seem a bit strange to you to find the Creed talking about believing in the "holy" Church. We are always hearing and reading news stories about the many weaknesses and imperfections in the Church. There are serious disagreements among people who belong to the same Church, those who claim to follow Jesus' teaching are divided up into a number of different churches. Maybe the priests and other ministers in your Church aren't even very inspiring examples of anything you would call "holiness," and all those gifts of the Spirit that Paul speaks about may not be too evident to you.

The Holiness of the Church

Of course, we know that if the Church as we experience it isn't a place of holiness, then that group of Christians aren't living up to what the Gospel calls them to be. But the Creed says more to us than that. It says that we believe in the holiness of the Church. And that doesn't mean shutting our eyes to the failings of our particular Church as though they didn't exist. But it does mean that we don't believe the types of stories which try to use the weaknesses in our Church to get us to say that religion is "no good" or "doesn't matter."

What makes the Church "holy"? You might think that having lots of good people as part of the Church would be the reason we speak of it as holy. But that would mean that the holiness of the Church would be changed by some measures of how bad or good Christians were at a particular time.

God's Holy Ones: The Saints

The New Testament writers knew that the holiness of the Church really came from God. This part of our Creed is related to the previous one, belief in the Holy Spirit. We believe that the Church is "holy" because through the Church the Holy Spirit is brought to the world. The earliest Christians sometimes used the expression "saints," which means "holy ones," to speak about Christians in general.

Here is how St. Paul began his words to the Christians at Rome: "To all God's beloved in Rome, called saints, grace to you and peace from God our Father and our Lord Jesus Christ" (Rom 1:7). When Paul speaks of someone as "called," he is not thinking just of sticking a name on someone. "Called" in Paul usually means when God called the person to become a Christian. Paul is thinking of God calling us to be Christians and to live a life of holiness.

Another beautiful example of the ''holiness'' of the Church comes from 1 Peter. This letter was written from Rome to Christians in rural Asia Minor. These Christians were being ridiculed and persecuted by their neighbors for just being Christian (see 1 Pet 4:16). They are told that when they became Christians in baptism they bound themselves to lead a life of holiness just like the holiness that God commanded the people to have in the Old Testament: ''As the one who called you [God] is holy, be holy yourselves, since it is written [in Lev 11:44–45], 'You shall be holy as I am holy'' (1 Pet 1:15–16).

Then the author goes on to tell the Christians that they are now the holy people of God. Before they became Christians they had been pagans completely separated from God. But now they have a new life as the holy people. And, if they are faithful, they may even convert some of their hostile neighbors:

> But you are a chosen race, a royal priesthood, a holy nation, God's own people, that you may declare the wonderful deeds of him who called you out of darkness into his marvelous light. Once you were no people but now you are God's people; once you had not received mercy but now you have received mercy. Beloved, I beseech you as aliens and exiles to abstain from the passions of the flesh that wage war against your soul. Maintain good conduct among the pagans, so that in case they speak against you as evildoers, they may see your good deeds and glorify God on the day of judgment (1 Pet 2:9–12).

Well, you get the idea by now. God is the one who is really holy and is the source of all holiness. The Church is holy because it is God's people. God has ''chosen'' or ''called'' people to a special life in that community. Of course, you can also see that we have a responsibility for holiness ourselves. 1 Peter reminds us that this responsibility is really a way of thanking God for our faith and salvation.

What We Must Do as Christians

1 Peter also reminds us of some of the responsibilities we have as members of a Church of holiness. We have to overcome the influence of all sorts of bad desires and habits in our lives. We have to be willing to witness to our belief in God and in Christ even when people say bad things about us for doing that. Later on in the letter 1 Peter reminds the Christians that they have to remember that they are not to retaliate against evil or hostility. Jesus' own teaching had put "love of enemies" together with the Old Testament idea of the Christian imitating the mercy or perfection of God (see Mt 5:48; Lk 6:36). So, if we really believe that the Church is holy, then we must also try to live in a way that shows others the holiness of the Church.

Christian Marriage and How We Love the Church

Our final example of the "holiness" of the Church comes from another letter in the Pauline tradition, the Letter to the Ephesians. The passage is really about marriage. The writer wants us to see that Christian marriages are different from others because the love between the husband and wife is to be based on the sacrifice of Christ for the "beloved Church." Christ's sacrifice makes the holiness of the Church possible.

People today often reject this passage because it talks about "being subject to one another" rather than about being independent and free to do what you want. You will notice that the reasons for the respect shown to the husband by the wife has nothing to do with making women "less equal." It is based on the love and sacrifice that is shown by the Christian husband. We should probably use that idea as a basis for respecting and obeying all sorts of people. You don't just obey because they are stronger or bigger. You respect people for what they give up and sacrifice to help others. And if you want others to respect you, then you have to show a similar attitude.

Ephesians says that Christ sacrificed himself so that the Church could be holy before God:

> Be subject to one another out of reverence for Christ. Wives, be subject to your husbands as to the Lord. For the husband is head of the wife as Christ is head of the Church, his body, and is himself its Savior. As the Church is subject to Christ, so let wives be subject in everything to their husbands.
>
> Husbands, love your wives as Christ loved the Church and gave himself up for her, that he might sanctify her, having cleansed her by the washing of water with the word, that he might present the Church to himself in splendor, without spot or wrinkle or any such thing that she might be holy and without blemish.
>
> Even so husbands should love their wives as their own bodies. He who loves his wife loves himself. For no man ever hates his own flesh, but nourishes it and cherishes it as Christ does the Church, because we are members of his body. "For this reason a man shall leave his father and mother and be joined to his wife, and the two shall become one" (Gen 2:24). This is a great mystery—I mean Christ and the Church; however, let each of you love his wife as himself, and let the wife see that she respects her husband (Eph 5:21–33).

This section of the New Testament reminds us that the Church is something special. It's not just some big, human institution. It's the object of Christ's love and sacrifice. The Church doesn't claim to be holy on its own. It claims that holiness comes from Christ's gift of himself so that people could become holy and cleansed from sin. The writer compares this relationship to the love between a man and woman—but not just any passion that we might call love. Ephesians is thinking of the love that leads a person to give up family and take another person as husband or wife to care for and live with that person forever.

This passage is a challenge to us. It challenges us to think about what it really means to love someone in Christian marriage. But it also challenges us to "love the Church" as much as Christ does. That may sound hard with all the negative stories about the Church and people in it that you hear around. But think about it. If someone criticizes your parents, or your brothers or sisters, or someone else you love, don't you stick up for that person? You might even agree that the person being criticized isn't perfect, but you still won't let the critic get away with putting down the people you love. Well, you can think of loving the Church as something like that. The holiness and perfection of the Church comes from God and Christ and the working of the Holy Spirit. But that doesn't mean that the people who make up the Church are perfect. We don't always live up to the holiness of the Church. Nevertheless, we can and should "love the Church" just as much as we love ourselves. And we should be willing to stick up for the Church if necessary too.

The Church Is Universal

In addition to saying that the Church is "holy" we also speak of the Church as "catholic." Sometimes we forget that "catholic" means "universal." We only think of "catholic" as "Roman Catholic," distinct from other groups of Christians.

Why is it important to believe that the Church is "catholic"?

Maybe it even seems evident to us that the Church is universal when we find Christians in every corner of the globe. You can even find them in the Soviet Union and in Communist China despite years of attempts by the government to teach people that religion is not necessary to their lives in a socialist state.

But the idea of the universality of the Church was quite a new one in the New Testament times. In those days, most countries had their own forms of religion. You belonged to whatever religion was traditional in your country. When people moved around the Roman empire, they took their local gods with them. But they did not try to convert people who were not from the same country to worshiping the gods they brought along. If Christianity had followed that route, then it would simply be a version of Judaism. After all, Jesus and his followers were all Jews, and Christianity was born in the homeland of the Jews.

But, inspired by Jesus' own example of reaching out to all people, the early Christians preached the Gospel to all people, whether they were Jewish or not. The passage from 1 Peter showed the thankfulness of non-Jewish Christians that they could now come to know the true God and be God's people.

The Jews and the Early Christians

Of course, there was opposition to this policy. Some of the earliest Christians were very devout Jews. They objected to the universal missionary work of people like Paul. They said that anyone who wanted to be a Christian had to become a Jew at the same time. They also said that Paul was turning Jewish Christians against the religion and customs of their ancestors (see Acts 21:17–21).

The Great Commission

The New Testament stories show us that God intends the Church to be universal. St. Paul tells us that a revelation of the risen Jesus turned him from persecuting the Christians to preaching the message among the Gentiles (those who are not Jews—Gal 1:13–17). The Gospel of Matthew concludes with the risen Lord telling his disciples to take the message into the whole world:

> And Jesus came and said to them, "All authority in heaven and on earth has been given to me. Go therefore and make disciples of all nations, baptizing them in the name of the Father and of the Son and of the Holy Spirit, teaching them to observe all that I have commanded you; and lo, I am with you always, to the close of the age" (Mt 28:18–20).

Non-Jewish Converts

Acts 10:1—11:18 preserves a story of the first non-Jewish converts baptized by St. Peter. If you read through that story, you will see that the Holy Spirit had to show Peter and the first disciples that it was God's will for the pious Roman centurion Cornelius and his household to be baptized and made part of the Church. You might also notice that Cornelius had been trying to know God even before Peter was sent to him. He had been praying to God and had been giving alms to the poor (Acts 10:2). He had also surrounded himself with other people who were looking for God.

The story tells us that at first Peter didn't want to go to Cornelius' home. The law had told pious Jews that they could not eat certain "unclean" foods and that they could not associate with pagans. These rules were a way of showing that the Jews were a specially chosen people set apart for God. So Peter learns something in the process. He finds out that God does not look at the ethnic, national or racial divisions between people. God looks for the people who are good and who are seeking to know God (Acts 10:34). God shows that the pagan Cornelius is just as good in God's sight as Jesus' own disciples by doing an extraordinary thing. God sends the Holy Spirit to Cornelius and his household even before they are baptized (10:44–46; 11:15–17).

This story about Cornelius does not mean that a person has not become a valid Christian until he or she has experienced such a manifestation of the Spirit. Nor does it replace baptism in the Lord's name as the way of entering the Christian community. Cornelius and his whole household are baptized by Peter. But this story does show us how important the ''catholic'' side of the Church is. God seeks out all people so that their hopes can be answered by salvation in Jesus.

The Challenge of the Universal Church

Peter is also a good example for us. He realizes that he has to give up his prejudice against Gentiles. And when he gets back to Jerusalem, he also has to defend what he has done before the other leaders of the Church. They, too, give up their objections and start praising God for inspiring repentance among the Gentiles.

You can see that believing in the ''catholic'' Church is quite a challenge. We have to work to overcome any kind of prejudice that keeps others from being part of our Christian community. We have to work to see that the good news about Jesus is preached everywhere in the world. And we have to remember that the Church includes Christians of other nations and races on the same basis as it includes us. We have all received the same baptism, the same Spirit, the same forgiveness from our sins. We all serve the same God and the same Lord, Jesus Christ.

The Communion of Saints

This part of our Creed emphasizes another aspect of the universal Church. The word "communion" means two things. It points to a fellowship, a bond of sharing between all who ever belong to the Church. And we also use it for the special bond between Christians and God that is established in the Eucharist. When this Creed was originally written, the Greek and Latin words that we translate "saints" could also mean "holy things." It is clear that the original authors meant for us to think of both sides at once. We are to think of ourselves as united to all other Christians, living and dead, and we are to think of ourselves as persons who share in the "holy things," the sacraments of the Church, especially the Eucharist.

The Church's Early Practices

The connection between the unity of all Christians and sharing the Lord's Supper (Eucharist) goes back to earliest times. In the very earliest Church, the Eucharist was celebrated as part of a full meal. People in ancient times were very conscious about proper rank and behavior at meals. A rich man might invite a large group for dinner but he would not treat everyone equally. His special friends would recline on couches near him and would receive the best food and wine. Others would be left to sit further away and would often be served inferior food.

Celebration of the Lord's Supper

St. Paul found out that in the Christian Church at Corinth the rich Christians who hosted the Lord's Supper were behaving in the same way. The rich Christians would go ahead with their own meal, eating and drinking, while the poor Christians would have nothing. Paul accuses those who behave in this way of "despising the Church of God" (1 Cor 11:22).

The first thing that Paul does is to remind the Corinthians of the special words of consecration. The Lord's Supper is not just any meal at which you have a good time. These are the words over the bread and wine as they were spoken at Corinth around A.D. 55:

> For I received from the Lord what I also delivered to you, that the Lord Jesus on the night when he was betrayed took bread, and when he had given thanks, he broke it and said, "This is my body which is for you. Do this in remembrance of me." In the same way, also the cup, after the supper, saying, "This cup is the new covenant in my blood. Do this as often as you drink it, in remembrance of me." For as often as you eat this bread and drink this cup, you proclaim the Lord's death until he comes (1 Cor 11:23–26).

You can see that when the Lord's Supper was originally celebrated the words over the bread and cup were separated, with the cup coming at the end of the meal. Some people think that at Corinth the two special actions had been put together at the end of the meeting. Paul goes on to tell the Corinthians that they are to wait for one another before they begin (1 Cor 11:33). The poorer Christians, many tradesmen and slaves, would not have been able to get away for the meal as the rich would. But it seems unlikely that the Corinthians would have deprived them of the sacramental part of the meal. Probably the Corinthians left that to the end. Meantime, the rich friends of the person whose house was being used would have already started banqueting and, Paul says, some of them even got drunk.

The Corinthians probably thought that what they were doing was all right because everyone received the bread and wine, "Communion," the body and blood of Christ. St. Paul tells them that they are "guilty of not recognizing the body of the Lord." That is because of the other sense of "communion," fellowship or sharing. St. Paul thinks of the Church as the "body of Christ." We become part of the body of Christ when we are baptized. We also share in the body of Christ when we receive Communion.

Communion: Partaking of the Body of Christ

But since all who share in that Communion are part of the body of Christ, it is wrong to act as the Corinthians did. They are not treating the poor members of the community as real members of the "body of Christ." They are simply treating them according to the social prejudices of their time. That is wrong. The Eucharist celebrates Christ offering himself for all. Paul even tells the Corinthians that they had better change, or they will face God's judgment for what they are doing.

Another example of how the first Christians put the "communion of saints" into practice occurs in the early community in Jerusalem. Acts 2:41–46 tells us about the great enthusiasm and sharing among the first converts:

So those who received his word were baptized . . . and they devoted themselves to the apostles' teaching and fellowship, the breaking of bread and prayers. . . . And all who believed were together and had all things in common; and they sold their possessions and goods and distributed them to all, as any had need. And day by day, attending the temple together and breaking bread in their homes, they partook of food with glad and generous hearts.

Unity of the Saints

Of course not all Christians could sell everything and live in common. But Acts puts this example right at the beginning to show us what the "communion of saints" really could mean. We enter the Church in baptism. The reality of our fellowship is expressed in the shared prayer of thanksgiving and in the Lord's Supper. In addition, Christians show their thankfulness in caring for one another and working to provide for the needs of those who are poor.

Eternal Union with the Lord

These examples of "communion" all refer to the experiences of fellowship between Christians who are living and who share the Lord's Supper together. But there is one more meaning to the phrase. It refers to the fact that the bond between Christians and the Lord that is the basis of "communion" continues beyond death.

The image of the Church as "body of Christ" used in Ephesians pictures Christ as head of the "whole body," that is, the Church spread throughout the whole world and all time. We are united to all Christians who have ever lived. Sometimes we forget that when we face separation or death. The Christians in Thessalonica, a city in northern Greece, forgot about that. St. Paul wrote and told them that they should not be sad and grieve like the non-Christians "who have no hope." He reminded them that Jesus will bring all those who have died with him at the resurrection of the dead. We would be united with them. Then the great fellowship of all Christians would be established "with the Lord" (1 Thess 4:13–18).

Because we believe that the "communion of saints" is universal, we are able to pray for Christians everywhere. We are able to offer special prayers of remembrance and thanksgiving for Christians who have died. And we are able to ask especially holy Christians, "the saints," who are now "with God," to aid us with their prayers.

The Forgiveness of Sins

We believe that the Church is "holy." Part of that holiness comes from the power to "forgive sins." In that way, those who have turned away from God can find God's love and forgiveness again. The Gospels tell us that Jesus "forgave sins" when he healed people of crippling diseases (Mk 2:1–12). After his resurrection, Jesus gave the power to forgive sins to the disciples (Jn 20:23). The basic message that they preached to the world was that people could turn to God and their sins would be forgiven. On Pentecost, Peter told the crowd, "Repent and be baptized, every one of you, in the name of Christ Jesus for the forgiveness of your sins; and you will receive the gift of the Holy Spirit" (Acts 2:38).

Baptism: Where God's Forgiveness Begins

The first place that Christians experience the power of forgiveness is in baptism. Since most early Christians were baptized as adults, baptism meant putting an old, sinful past behind them. But they also recognized that the power of forgiveness could not stop with baptism. As long as Christians live in a world marked by imperfection, human sinfulness and large-scale evils that do not seem to be the fault of any one person, Christians need to ask God's forgiveness.

The early Christians realized that Jesus, their Savior, was in heaven with God. Jesus had suffered for us and would not abandon us now. The Jewish people have a day of fasting and repentance every year. They call it Yom Kippur, "the day of atonement." The Christians realized that their "day of atonement" was possible "every day" because Christ was their sacrifice. Christ now lives in heaven to pray for the Christian people.

The Christian understanding of sin is more radical than that suggested by atonement for the sins of individuals or the people as a whole. When Paul reflects upon the long story of humans turning away from God in Romans 1:18—3:20, he observes that all human beings, even the Jews who had the advantage of God's revelation in the Commandments, stand before God as sinners. Without Christ's salvation no one could claim to be righteous. In Romans 5:12–17 Paul traces this universal sinfulness back to the sin of the father of the human race, Adam. God had given Adam and Eve all the blessings of paradise. But they had to obey his command not to touch the fruit of a single tree (Gen 2:15—3:24). Their disobedience brought sinfulness, death and suffering upon all who are descended from them. Thus, Paul can say that all people, from the very beginning, are implicated in sin. But Paul also knows that the freedom from sin that comes with Christ as the "new Adam" means freedom from this "original sin" as well as forgiveness for individual sins. That is why Paul can also speak of the person who has become part of Christ through baptism and the Spirit as a "new creation" (2 Cor 5:17; Gal 6:15). That is also why we can speak of baptism bringing "freedom from sin" to a baby even though the baby has not yet personally turned away from God by some act of sin.

Confession: Where God's Forgiveness Continues

The author of the Letter to the Hebrews speaks of Christ as a heavenly "high priest" who is always there to help us. Even though Christ is "in heaven," he sympathizes with our weaknesses and problems because he is fully human. Hebrews encourages Christians to pray to Christ for help:

> Since we have a great high priest, who has passed through the heavens, Jesus Christ, the Son of God, let us hold fast to our confession. For we have not a high priest who is unable to sympathize with our weaknesses, but one who in every way has been tempted as we are, yet without sin. Let us then draw near to the throne of grace with confidence, that we may receive mercy and find grace to help in time of need (Heb 4:14–16).

The author of 1 John wrote about confession of sin in a different context. Some Christians were claiming that Christians did not commit sin. 1 John tells his readers that such claims are self-deception. Christians should confess their sins. They can be sure of God's mercy because they have Jesus Christ praying for them in heaven:

> If we say we have no sin, we deceive ourselves, and the truth is not in us. If we confess our sins, he [God] is faithful and just and will forgive our sins and cleanse us from all unrighteousness. . . . My little children, I am writing this to you so that you may not sin; but if any one does sin, we have an advocate with the Father, Jesus Christ, the righteous; and he is the expiation for our

sin, and not for ours only but also for the sins of the whole world (1 Jn 1:8—2:2).

Why Pray for Others?

Later on in the letter, 1 John tells Christians that they should pray for others who are sinners so that the sinner can receive forgiveness:

If anyone sees his fellow Christian committing what is not a mortal sin, he will ask, and God will give life to the one whose sin is not mortal. There is sin which is mortal; I do not say that one is to pray for that. All wrongdoing is sin, but there is sin which is not mortal (1 Jn 5:16–17).

Beware of False Teachings

1 John does not make it clear what kind of sin "leads to death" and cannot be forgiven. But much of the letter warns the readers against a group of people who have separated from the Johannine Church and who no longer share fellowship and love with their fellow Christians. Most scholars think that 1 John has those persons in mind. They have deliberately turned away from the teaching of Christ. They have deliberately turned against the community of Christians which has possessed that teaching from the beginning. They do not follow the fundamental Christian command of love. 1 John 2:18–19 and 4:2–5 identify such teaching with the anti-christ.

Forgiveness Through Jesus

These examples do not tell us exactly how forgiveness of sins was celebrated in the earliest Church. But they show that Christians knew that forgiveness comes to us through Jesus. Jesus knows our difficulties and weaknesses. They should not stand between us and God. But we have to make the effort. We have to keep turning back to him for help and forgiveness.

Loving Others, Knowing God

In addition, we see that forgiveness is not just a private matter between each person and God. Most of our sins are not private matters either. 1 John makes the whole life of the Christian depend upon loving others. That is the only way to show that we really do "know God." And we see that forgiveness is received in community prayer for the person who has sinned.

These basic elements are part of all of our celebrations of penance. We must acknowledge that in sinning we have failed to be faithful to God's teaching. We have not shown the kind of love for others that Jesus taught. We must also pray for forgiveness. When we make such prayers, we are certain of being heard. The forgiveness we receive should not lead us to think that God is a "pushover" or a "soft touch," something kids sometimes say about their parents.

Return to God

The reason we receive forgiveness in penance is that Jesus loves us so much that he was willing to take on suffering for us, in our place. Jesus wants to see us turn back to God and be united with God again. We can keep on trying as much as we need to. The "deadly" sin is committed by the person who deliberately throws out God. So we have to give some sign that we really are trying to come back to God and that we really do want to receive God's love and mercy.

Public Confession of Sins

Finally, forgiveness is the task of the Church. We see that Christians are to pray for one another. It's not quite enough to think in private that you're sorry you did something bad. You also have to admit that publicly, to the community. Of course, today, the public part of penance may be pretty private, just you and the priest who is representing the Church. But even that does make you look and see that you really have done something to be sorry about. You are making a promise to the community to try to follow Jesus better in the future. The sacrament of penance is not just a matter of your inner resolve to turn away from sin and be better in the future. The priest, when he gives you absolution, has the power to speak God's forgiveness. This word of forgiveness will be upheld even at the judgment (see Mt 16:19). Penance is much more than our individual promises to be better or some form of counseling session; it is an opportunity to really receive God's forgiveness.

"Is Any Among You Sick?"

Our last example of forgiveness and confession of sin in the Church comes from the Letter of James. There it is connected with another sacrament, the anointing of the sick. Jesus' own healing ministry had linked healing and forgiveness of sin. In James 5:13–16, the author speaks of the different kinds of prayer in the Church. The "elders" of the community are to come and pray for the sick person:

Is anyone among you suffering? Let him pray. Is anyone cheerful? Let him sing praise. Is anyone among you sick? Let him call for the elders of the Church, and let them pray over him, anointing him with oil in the name of the Lord, and the prayer of faith will save the sick person, and the Lord will raise him up; and if he has committed sins, he will be forgiven. Therefore confess your sins to one another, and pray for one another, that you may be healed.

This passage puts the anointing of the sick right in the center of its general teaching on Christian prayer and forgiveness. The ordained leaders of the community, the "elders," are called to anoint the sick person and to pray over that person. The person will receive forgiveness for any sins committed. And, as in Jesus' ministry, the faith expressed in such prayer is part—together with the power of Christ in the sacrament—of a healing process for the sick person.

It had become the custom to summon the priest to anoint a person only when that person was near death. Even today some people who are seriously ill do not want to receive the anointing of the sick because they think it means they are going to die. But the Church has been trying to show people that the sacrament of anointing of the sick is an important part of the life of the Christian. It represents part of the healing ministry of the Church. Anyone who is very sick should be happy to call on a priest to receive this sacrament. Maybe you'll have to have an operation someday. You could ask to be anointed before your operation. Hopefully, the experience of God's love and care for you in this sacrament would help you be a little less scared. You are not being left "all alone" with no one to help you.

The Sacraments: Expressions of the Church's Holiness

You can see that the various expressions of forgiveness play a big role in the life of the Christian. You can also see that the "holiness" of the Church is experienced in a number of ways through special actions which the Church calls "sacraments." You come into the community of "the saints" when you first receive God's grace and the Spirit in baptism. When you are old enough to be responsible for your Christian faith yourself, the laying on of hands and anointing at confirmation brings you a special gift of grace to be a witness to the Gospel.

The Eucharist: Experiencing Christ's Salvation Now

We celebrate our salvation through Christ and express our unity as a Christian people in the Eucharist, the Lord's Supper. Christ's salvation continues to be present in the Eucharist. And we shouldn't think of going to Mass as some sort of unpleasant duty forced on us out of fear. We are there to remember what Christ went through for us. We are there to be united with Christ and with all other Christians so that we can lead the Christian life. And most of all, we are there to "give thanks"—that's what the word "Eucharist" means—for all the love God has given us.

Marriage: Experiencing God's Love

Married Christians are also shown that they can experience the love and holiness of God in marriage. But they have to remember that marriage is not just a legal arrangement. It's a "sacrament," a sign and source of God's grace. The love and sacrifice required in marriage is no less than the love and sacrifice of Christ himself.

Holy Orders: The Guides of God's Church

The example from James shows that some members of the community, "the elders," had special authority. Elsewhere in the New Testament we learn that elders were "installed" by the laying on of hands after a period of preparation that involved prayer and fasting (Acts 14:23). In other churches, the leaders were called "episcopoi," "overseers," a word that we usually translate "bishops." They were assisted in their work by "deacons," a word derived from the general Greek word of serving or ministering (1 Tim 3:1–13). Women may also have served as deacons (1 Tim 3:11).

The primary responsibilities of the "elders" or the "overseers" was to guide and administer the affairs of the local community. The New Testament also speaks of "teachers" and "prophets" in the community. James 3:1 warns people that those who are "teachers" will be held responsible for what they teach. 1 Peter 5:1–4 reminds the "elders" that they have to follow Jesus' example in the way they take care of those in their flock. They should not be grudging about their task. They should not be domineering. They should not be out to get money for it. Instead, they have to set an example by taking Jesus for their model.

Eventually, these different Church offices would become the "bishops, priests and deacons" that we have today. The Church sets the requirements for being "ordained" to these ministries and the role which the ordained minister plays in celebrating the different sacraments. The fundamental tasks remain those of guiding the community, of representing the community in the larger world, of teaching and preaching the Gospel, of celebrating the Eucharist and other sacraments and of overseeing all that needs to be done to "care for" all who are part of the Church. Of course, those tasks are much too large to be handled just by the clergy. We are all called upon in different ways to share the larger ministry of the Church in serving the Gospel and one another.

In addition, there are many lay people and religious working full-time in the Church's ministry who are not ordained. Some of these ministries require special training. Sometimes we have a special prayer service to "commission" people who are devoting themselves in ministries in our churches. They are an important part of helping the Church be the "holy people of God."

The Healing Sacraments

Finally, the sacraments of penance and anointing of the sick are important to the "holiness" of the Church and to its desire to heal and bring God closer to people. We do not deny that we are imperfect Christians. We do not deny that Christians are often sick and suffering. But we also believe that Jesus' sacrifice and love for us means that sin, suffering and even death are not the end of everything. Our answer to sinfulness is to repent, to always be ready to turn back to God. We know that Jesus is there to help us. In suffering and sickness, we also look to God with confidence in God's care for us. The Church is not holy because we Christians are perfect. The holiness of the Church always comes as a gift from God's love in Jesus Christ.

8

Resurrection and Eternal Life

*the resurrection of the flesh
and eternal life.*

The Resurrection of the Flesh

The conclusion of the Creed reminds us of the goal that awaits all faithful Christians, a share in the life of the risen Lord. We have already seen what "resurrection" means to people in Jesus' time in Chapter Four. Resurrection of the flesh, the physical body, did not mean some sort of vampire existence in which the corpse would come out of the grave. No, it meant a glorious change in the body so that it could share heavenly glory.

What Will Our Bodies Be Like?
We learned that Jesus rejected those who thought that "resurrection of the flesh" was a stupid idea. He told them that they

simply didn't understand the "power of God." They should realize that life in the resurrection would not be like life in our bodies here on earth. They should know that God as Creator has
power over life and death.

But we probably still have a hard time believing that. Once
when I was young, we had a pet turtle which died. So my brothers
and sisters and I decided to give it a funeral in the yard. We
wrapped the turtle up, took out a prayer book with the funeral service in it and buried the turtle. A few days later, my mother found
one of my brothers digging away where we had buried the turtle.
He wanted to know what had happened to the turtle's body. Naturally, she made him fill in the hole and tried to explain to him
that the soft part would rot away leaving the shell after a few
weeks.

My brother was pretty small at the time, so he didn't go back
to dig up the shell. My sister and I, who were older, thought he
was pretty dumb to try to dig up the turtle anyway. But sometimes
even grown-ups can't help thinking that "resurrection of the
flesh" is like my brother and the turtle. But, instead of a shell,
we'll all come out walking around again.

We can't help thinking like that because we are trying to
imagine something that isn't like anything we ever experience in
this world. We know what happens to dead bodies in this world.
And even people who take elaborate efforts to preserve the body
with embalming, like the ancient Egyptian mummies, really can't
change the natural way that living things die.

The Teaching on the Resurrection

St. Paul ran up against this problem in Corinth. The Christians there weren't at all sure that they believed in resurrection.
First Paul reminds them of the Creed. He points out that if God

didn't raise Jesus from the dead, then the whole Christian message is a lie.

But Paul goes on to point out that Jesus' resurrection is much more than a special reward for Jesus. It is the beginning of something new, life for all those who are brothers and sisters of Jesus. The death and resurrection of Christ was a victory over death. But that victory would be no good if it just left humanity the same as before. No, death is going to be destroyed when all those who belong to Christ are raised up like Christ (1 Cor 15:12–27).

St. Paul says that those people who ask what kind of body the resurrected people will have are fools. They should think of the relationship between the body we have now and that we will have in the resurrection as something like the relationship between the dried-up seed you plant and the flourishing wheat or other grain that grows from it. Our risen body, he says, will be a spiritual, heavenly one like that of Christ (1 Cor 15:35–50). One of the major differences between it and bodies as we know them is that it won't ever change. It can't be weak or sick or have cancer or decay or die. Since this resurrected body is so different from anything we know, we can't get a clear picture of what it would be like.

Why Believe in the Resurrection of the Flesh?

Why bother insisting on resurrection of the body, then? Part of the answer lies in our tradition. We believe that God raised all of Jesus from the dead. The Lord we worship in heaven is the Jesus who lived here on earth and who was crucified. The risen Lord is not just some "inner part" of that Jesus which never really belonged to this world. We also believe that what God did for Jesus, God will do for us. St. Paul told the Corinthians that they would be transformed into the likeness of the risen Christ.

There is also another reason for believing in the resurrection of the body which may be easier for you to understand. It really isn't possible to think of who we would be without including some idea of our body. Just try it. Can you imagine who you are without thinking of some images or experiences that are connected with your body? Pretty hard, isn't it?

If the most important things that happen to us are connected with our body, then the body should also have a share in salvation. So even if we can't say much about what a resurrected body would be like, we can say what we would be like. We can say that everything important about us as individuals is part of the risen body. You really will be yourself at the resurrection.

Treat Your Body as Something Holy

St. Paul also realized that if we believe the body shares in salvation, we have to treat the body like something holy. Being a good person is not just located in your mind somewhere; it is also part of how you use your body.

Some people think that the Holy Spirit only comes into a person's soul somewhere. But St. Paul tells the Christians at Rome that the Spirit which dwells in the Christian is the same Spirit that raised Jesus from the dead. It dwells in us and will be responsible for our resurrection. That means we have to live like people of the Spirit and not just follow whatever our desires of the moment are (Rom 8:5–11).

St. Paul found that he had problems with some Christians who thought that it didn't matter what they did with their bodies as long as they were united to God with their soul. Some of the Christians in Corinth argued that it was all right to have sex with prostitutes. They argued that the body was going to die anyway, so it didn't matter what you did with it. Paul rejects that idea. He thinks that sexual morality is particularly important because that involves your body in the act. Sex should be part of Christian marriage where it can serve as an image of Christ. Otherwise you are just turning away from Christ to make yourself part of something else. Paul challenges the Corinthians. He tells them that they are taking what belongs to Christ and making it part of a prostitute.

Throughout this argument, St. Paul keeps reminding the Corinthians that the body is the temple of the Holy Spirit. The body is going to be raised up. We cannot abuse our bodies if we believe in resurrection of the body.

It may be pretty hard to think about how you treat your body as important to your religion. Our society gives us lots of different messages about the body. Ads encourage us to pamper the body and give it everything it desires. Many young people, especially girls, become so worried about what their bodies look like that they won't eat anymore. Or they may gorge themselves and then throw up so they won't get fat. It sometimes takes a lot of work with counselors and doctors to get over eating disorders like that.

If you are planning a career as an athlete, you may get a different message about your body. You have to work out to build it up. But you are also told to play with pain. The only thing that counts is winning the game. You have to give everything for the team.

Not long ago, I was talking to one of the starters on our college's championship football team. He was pretty "beat up" just from five scrimmages a week during spring practices. Other guys were out practicing with real injuries. After all, they could use the summer to get over them. The boy I was talking to said, "They train you to totally forget your body. No wonder so many athletes wind up on drugs. By the time you're a star, you no longer listen to anything your body says." Well, that's not a Christian attitude to the body either.

The boy I was talking to is also a serious Christian. He is able to see that he has to take care of his body as best he can no matter what the pressures are. He doesn't think that it's "cool" to sleep with lots of girls or get drunk or take drugs. That doesn't make him a boring person even though some people may kid him. He also likes to be with the other students, go to parties and have a good time. He has a lot of sympathy for the guys who go too far because he knows how easy that is, especially for a star athlete.

So you can see that believing in the resurrection of the body is pretty important after all. Do you really treat your body as though it were "part of Christ"? Do you really treat your body as something good and holy, something to take care of? Or do you follow the crowd and treat your body as a thing to be used any old way you want?

Belief in Eternal Life

The final sentence of the Creed reminds us of another important belief, eternal life. When we are young, it seems as though this life is going to go on forever. Maybe you can't wait to grow up or to get your driver's license or your first car. So it may not seem too important to worry about whether or not this life is all there is.

But if someone close to you dies or a kid in school gets killed in a car accident, then maybe things change a bit. This life doesn't seem quite so "endless" after all. We have already seen that Christians do not believe that this life is it. They believe that people who have loved and served God will live forever joined together with the Lord.

Death Is Not To Be Feared

The Christian should not fear death and mourn in the same way that others do. St. Paul told the Christians at Thessalonica, "We do not want you to be ignorant, brothers, about those who are asleep [dead], so that you may not mourn as other people do who have no hope'' (1 Thess 4:13). Of course, Paul knows that we will be sad when someone dies. He knows that we will miss that person. We may even be angry. This morning's paper had a story of a thirteen year old boy named Todd who was a New England champion tennis player and who was killed by a drunk driver as he was on his way to get ice cream with his cousin.

The story, told by his father, was part of an ad to get people to take action against drunk driving. Of course, we are angry when something like that happens to a young person. Of course, Todd's family is hurt by what happened. His father said that he saw Todd everywhere.

Believing in eternal life does not make the sad story of someone's death go away. But it does tell us that for Todd that terrible death was not the end. Todd's dreams of becoming a baseball star or a tennis champion were cut off. Yet somehow, through God's power, we believe that Todd will be able to experience in an even greater way the happiness and the thrill that would have come if he had lived to be a champion.

Dying for Christ

Some of the earliest Christians had to show that they were not afraid of death in very dramatic ways. People were suspicious of Christianity because it wasn't like any of the religions they knew. Christians didn't go along with worshiping the gods and goddesses of the state. Christians would not make sacrifices honoring the Roman emperor as a god either.

Whenever local suspicions and hostility got too bad, some people would start to torture Christians. They might be beaten or thrown in jail, and many were even killed just for being Christians. They could have saved themselves by denying that they were Christians and making sacrifices to the emperor. Many of

Jesus' first disciples were put to death like St. Peter. St. Paul also was finally killed. He had been in jail and in danger of death many times before that. In fact, he tells the Corinthians that if he did not believe that he would be raised to life again, he would never have gone through what he did:

> Why am I in danger every hour? I protest, brothers, by the pride in you which I have in Christ Jesus our Lord, I die every day! What do I gain if, humanly speaking, I fought with the beasts at Ephesus? If the dead are not raised, "let us eat and drink for tomorrow we die" (1 Cor 15:30–32).

You will notice that Paul tells the Corinthians that a person has a choice. The person who is not afraid of death will risk anything for what he or she believes in. But the person who thinks that there is no eternal life can never do that. The person who thinks there is no eternal life can only live for pleasure. Paul is quoting a popular saying, "Let us eat and drink for tomorrow we die."

Death Is Not the End

If you really believe that death is the end of everything, then your attitude toward life will have to be completely selfish. You will do whatever makes you happy at the moment because there is no reason to do anything else. Sometimes young people who have that attitude do the most irrational thing of all—they kill themselves.

Maybe you've heard of someone who has done that. Maybe you or a friend of yours has even wondered if it wouldn't be easier just to end your life. I know a family that happened to. They had eight children. The oldest son killed himself when he was nineteen. No one knows why. He didn't leave any note. None of his friends had any idea that he was unhappy.

A few months ago, I found a birthday card that boy had made for me when he was small, maybe about eight. That card is a memory of a happier time, a promise of life that somehow went wrong. Naturally, his family and friends all wonder what they could have done. We won't ever know. We can hope that for all the kind things this boy had done in his life, maybe God can heal the terrible pain that must have made him do what he did.

But if you really believe in eternal life, you believe that it takes the goodness of your life here and makes it complete. Eternal life with God takes away the pain and suffering in joy and peace. You wouldn't want to cut off your life in pain or anger or despair if you thought that that might be how you would be forever.

Love Is Eternal

Most of us will never have to face anything that serious. Most of us will never be threatened with imprisonment or death just because we are Christians. But we can all show that we believe in eternal life by the way we live here and now. Christianity makes us people of joy and hope. We never give up. Belief in eternal life means that all our hopes and dreams are finally gathered up in God and in the love that never comes to an end. St. Paul wrote a beautiful summary of the Christian life of love:

Love is patient and kind; love is not jealous or boastful; it is not arrogant or rude; love is not irritable or resentful; it does not rejoice at wrong, but rejoices in the right. Love bears all things, believes all things, hopes all things, endures all things. Love never ends. . . . So faith, hope and love remain forever, these three; but the greatest of these is love (1 Cor 13:4–8, 13).

God Is Love

Everything that we do and believe as Christians is an expression of love because love is the nature of God:

God is love, and whoever abides in love, abides in God, and God abides in him (1 Jn 4:16).